BEYOND DEATH

ALSO BY HANS HOLZER

Fiction

The Alchemist
Heather, Confessions of a Witch
The Amityville Curse
The Secret of Amityville
The Zodiak Affairs
The Entry
The Clairvoyant
Circle of Love
The Adventures of Randy Knowles

Non-fiction

Tales at Midnight
Born Again
America's Mysterious Places
Healing Beyond Medicine
Haunted Hollywood
Star in the East
The New Pagans
Murder in Amityville
Hans Holzer's Haunted America

ALSO BY PHILIP SOLOMON

Ghosts, Legends, and Psychic Snippets
Black Country Ways in Bygone Days
Dreamer's Psychic Dictionary
Ghosts and Phantoms of Central England

BEYOND DEATH

Conditions in the Afterlife

PHILIP SOLOMON
and
Prof. HANS HOLZER, Ph.D.

HAMPTON ROADS
PUBLISHING COMPANY, INC.

Cover art and design by Marjoram Productions

For information write:

Hampton Roads Publishing Company, Inc.
1125 Stoney Ridge Road
Charlottesville, VA 22902

Or call: 804-296-2772
Fax: 804-296-5096
e-mail: hrpc@hrpub.com
www.hrpub.com

If you are unable to order this book from your local
bookseller, you may order directly from the publisher.
Call 1-800-766-8009, toll-free.

Library of Congress Catalog Card Number: 00-110246
ISBN 1-57174-202-6
10 9 8 7 6 5 4 3 2

Printed on acid-free paper in Canada

TABLE OF CONTENTS

Introduction by Professor Hans Holzer, Ph.D. ix

Chapter 1: Do We Ever Die? 1

Chapter 2: Philip Solomon Contacts Hans Holzer 7

Chapter 3: Investigating the Other Side 13

Chapter 4: David's Progression to the Higher Life 19

Chapter 5: Patrick's Story 26

Chapter 6: The Words of Father Thomas 30

Chapter 7: An Interview with the King, Elvis 33

Chapter 8: Interview with Dr. Roberts 36

Chapter 9: Interview with Richard Lewis 42

Chapter 10: Conversation with Peter Jackson 49

Chapter 11: Interview with Janet 54

Chapter 12: Conversation with George Smith 63

Chapter 13: The Words of Princess Diana 71

Chapter 14: Interview with May Thompson 76

Chapter 15: Michael's Communication 82

Chapter 16: Rosemary and Larry Visit the
Theater and Library 90

Chapter 17: The Spirit John and Philip Have a
Question-and-Answer Session 97

Chapter 18: A Communication between a Couple
Reunited in Spirit 109

Chapter 19: A Message from Rudolph Ovaraith 114

Chapter 20: Conversation with Mary of Medici 117

Chapter 21: Message from Theo 121

Chapter 22: Conversation with Lee Travers 125

Chapter 23: A Visit with Al Capone 131

Chapter 24: Interview with Judy Garland 139

Chapter 25: A Talk with Beryl Reid 144

Chapter 26: Conversation with Joanna 148

Chapter 27: Message from Franz 151

Chapter 28: Message from Johnny 155

Chapter 29: Interview with Jenny 160

Chapter 30: Message from the Spirit Paul 164

Chapter 31: Conversation with Maurice 167

Chapter 32: A Talk with the Spirit Sarah 176

Chapter 33: Message from Michael Bentine 181

Chapter 34: Conversation with Marlene Dietrich . . .186

Chapter 35: Adolph Hitler Speaks 191

Chapter 36: Message from Bernie Winters 196

Chapter 37: Marilyn Monroe Talks 202

Chapter 38: Conversation with Danny Kelly 207

Chapter 39: Conclusions
             by Professor Hans Holzer, Ph.D. 212

Index 215

INTRODUCTION

As a professional parapsychologist and investigator of paranormal events and claims, I meet all kinds of psychic people, those who have had experiences in their personal lives that needed an explanation, and professionals who wanted me to test them for accuracy in their work. There are three unacceptable terms in my professional vocabulary: belief, disbelief, and supernatural. "Belief" is the uncritical acceptance of something you can't prove objectively; "disbelief" is an *a priori* rejection without truly examining the facts, especially facts that, if proven, would tend to be unacceptable to the person involved; and "supernatural" does not exist since everything in all universes is of necessity natural, whether we understand it or not at any given moment in our time consciousness.

So I come to the subject of life after death with a great deal of caution, just as with any claim transcending or contrary to current scientific convictions.

There are those who have genuine evidence; and there are others who believe they have, but have not; and finally, there are some—though not as many as is often thought—who are conscious frauds in quest of a fast buck or attention.

Claims involving proof of life after death must therefore be of a kind that can withstand the most honest and even rigorous examination as to possible alternate explanations not requiring a suspension of conventional views regarding the nature of life and death. But scientific proof of such claims must not be perverted into disguised disbelief either, as so often happens with those who have not looked at the evidence from an objective point of view.

After a lifetime of involvement with psychical research, I have become sophisticated in my ability to distinguish between true and false claims and the gray area of unproven possibilities. When dealing with psychics and mediums—the latter being links to the Other Side of life, the dimension into which we all must pass on physical death—we need to look carefully at the circumstances under which a piece of alleged evidence is being offered.

Has the medium had any prior knowledge of the matter or person whose message is being offered? Is the information common knowledge and readily accessible? Not unlike a detective investigating a case of murder or other crime, we must ask ourselves such questions so as not to wind up deceived, either by the claimant or by ourselves.

Having known, worked with, and sometimes developed some of our best mediums and psychics, I always welcome "new talents" when they appear.

It was in the summer of 1995 that Philip Solomon became aware of me and my work for the first time, and I of him and his work. Both of us may be known in our own local environment, but some three thousand miles away from each other, that is not necessarily so. I haven't had a book published in England in years, so Philip could not have had easy access to information concerning me.

Philip Solomon happened to have been a subscriber to an American magazine called *Fate*. In fact, he had been complaining to the editors about the lateness of its arrival. When the July 1995 issue arrived in England, he found an article about the leading American mediums, and how to work with them, to be of great interest. The article had been written by me and laid down the strict rules of evidence I have always followed in respect to trance mediums and other psychics when it comes to the validity of evidence (of spirit communication) and other matters of professional conduct. My address was also listed in *Fate*.

Philip was so impressed with the piece, he wrote to me

commenting upon the validity of my approach to mediumship. I replied, and in turn asked him, of whom I knew nothing at that point, to send me some background material. At that time we had not yet met face to face, but there had been increasing correspondence and occasional telephone conversations between us, as my favorable impression of the quality of his work grew. Philip and I became long distance friends, and in time it became clear to me that his contacts with the Other Side were far different from others in that they contained more precise data that one usually gets from such communications.

Whenever Philip Solomon offered an item purporting to come from a dead relative or friend or person, my safeguard was always the question: Could he have had any access to this specific bit of information? Is there anything in this "message" that proves the origin of it? Is there any purpose to the message?

Having had, over the years, mediums amongst my friends who would send well-meaning but rather vague bits, allegedly from dead relatives, I naturally look for specifics to make the case for a genuine contact with the Other Side. Ever since we had contact, Philip never failed to amaze me with the accuracy and timeliness of these messages, and what he calls "snippets" of information from those living in the next world.

Once I had become totally convinced of the high accuracy of this material, it occurred to me to ask him to present to the general public a book exploring the kind of life people lead "over there" once they have shed their physical, outer bodies, and live on in their inner, etheric bodies.

This book is the result, and it is, as far as I know, the first time a methodical question-and-answer approach about life on the Other Side has been attempted, especially by a team consisting of an academic parapsychologist, like myself, approaching the material cautiously, uncommitted and open-minded, and a proven first-class medium like Philip Solomon.

That the conditions and details described in these pages represent the facts I have no doubts whatever. Some of the descriptions given by the people on the Other Side—communicating with the medium—I have heard before, and there is nothing revolutionary or startling in these revelations except that we have now, for the first time, a detailed, exact, descriptive picture of what life on the Other Side consists of. It supports bits and pieces about this subject I have known for years, and it dispels fanciful notions some people may have of a wonderful paradise or Heaven, or of fears of a terrible Hell down below somewhere.

The truth is different, and greater, and requires no faith or beliefs, only an understanding of a well-ordered universe beyond the physical level, and the absolute continuance of what we have come to call life.

—Prof. Hans Holzer, Ph.D.

CHAPTER 1

DO WE EVER DIE?

There is a great deal of interest, even amongst the conservative scientific community, regarding certain psychic phenomena that cannot be readily explained as falling within the context of recognized physical science. The number of researchers who tend to dismiss all such experiences as either hallucinations or fraudulent, or, at best, as misinterpretations, is dwindling rapidly as more evidence regarding another (or perhaps plural) dimension beyond our physical world is presented.

Enlightened and open-minded scientists will study phenomena and then draw conclusions regarding the laws governing such phenomena. Those clinging to nineteenth century materialistic concepts of the universe will do it the other way around: If the reported phenomena do not fit into pre-existing (and restrictive) laws, they cannot be valid!

The reason for this defensive position is obvious: If we accept as real certain natural phenomena of the psychic kind, including evidence for the survival of the human personality after bodily death, it affects our entire view of our world, our philosophy, our way of life. Many people prefer the comfort of the world they are familiar with to the new and as yet only partially understood world of multiple dimensions.

But that attitude is changing. People who have reported experiencing apparitions of the dead are not necessarily

1

always accused of hallucinating or sent to the nearest psychiatrist for possible commitment to an institution. The late Professor Hornell Hart of Duke University, in a survey of reported apparition cases, has stated: "In my view, the apparitions of the dead are indeed who they claim to be."

Stanley R. Dean, M.D., clinical professor of psychiatry at the University of Miami, Florida Medical School, states that "sufficient proof has been established for the existence of psychic phenomena, and now the current need is to disseminate the scientific basis of such phenomena." H.H. Price, Wykeham Professor of Logic, University of Oxford, in discussing whether people sometimes experience apparitions of the dead states: "They certainly do. No one who examines the evidence can come to any other conclusion."

Respected medical people now take an active interest in research in this area. Dr. Raymond Moody, author of *Life After Life;* the Swiss physician Dr. Elisabeth Kübler-Ross, author of *On Death and Dying* and other books, are pioneers in the field.

Because of the current political climate in which the Religious Right in America exercises pressures on even purely scientific matters when they contradict or tend to question established religious beliefs or traditions, it is not easy to be a pioneer in this area of inquiry. But the fact remains that parapsychology and religion have only one thing in common: The former validates the latter to a large extent. Faith has its place in human consciousness, of course, and a very important one indeed; but it is of a different order (or shall we say, dimension?) than enlightened, scientific research.

Properly documented, authenticated cases allowing no alternate explanation can be found in large numbers. Here are a few:

Don McIntosh of Richland, Washington, worked as a security guard most of his life, without the slightest interest in the paranormal. But on November 15, 1971, at 6:30 P.M., he woke up because of a feeling of some sort of "presence" in his room. Sure enough, there at the foot of his bed, he clearly saw the face of his cousin and heard him say, "Don, I have died!"

Mr. McIntosh, fully awake at the time, immediately recognized his cousin's voice, just as the face disappeared. He was puzzled, because, as far as he knew, his cousin was well and living a thousand miles away, in Ventura, California. Don and his wife discussed the matter, wondering whether they should contact the cousin. But three hours later, at 9:30 A.M., the mail brought a letter from the cousin's wife, informing them that he had died of heart failure at 9:30 P.M., November 8, 1971, a week before the incident had taken place.

Two questions of great impact present themselves once we are beyond the evidence for survival and/or communication itself. What exactly is it that survives the dissolution of the physical body? Is there really such a thing as "the soul" as religion would have us believe? It would seem that we exist in multiple layers: The heaviest, outer, layer being the body as we know it, and underneath it a finer, duplicate "body" in which our consciousness resides, and in which it continues the journey onward, once the outer, physical layer is no more. But where is the evidence?

Kirlian photography, developed by a Russian parapsychologist some years ago, has shown the so-called "life force" that leaves a leaf or plant when it dies. If man has an "inner tube" that survives physical death, then that, too, should be capable of observation; and so it is.

Mrs. C.M. Roche was living in New England with her husband, John, who had spent a lifetime working as a machinist at a leather factory. When he complained of chest pain, the doctor diagnosed it as pleurisy and told him to stay in bed; John was in no imminent danger and the doctor left. That night he complained of pain, and Mrs. Roche decided to keep a watchful eye on him all night long. Suddenly, she saw a "white robed figure" closely resembling her husband rise up from the bed and vanish. When she checked on her husband, he had died.

The other question we must ask ourselves, when dealing with evidence suggesting that the so-called dead can communicate both visually and auditorily with the living, is why, and under what exact conditions? From the vast pool of case material, it would appear that in the majority of cases there is some urgency, some need to make contact—such as letting the family know the deceased is "well and happy," or to address some unfinished business still disturbing the departed one who is supposed to be "resting in peace" according to traditional attitudes toward death . . . that it is the end of the road.

A particularly good case in point concerns a California-based scholar and teacher named Bernard Mollenhauer, whose mother, Frances Mollenhauer, a gifted music teacher, died suddenly of a stroke at age forty-two. As requested in her will, she was to be cremated and her ashes placed in a niche at Greenwood Cemetery. Mollenhauer left town after the funeral and thought no more about it. But a month later his mother appeared to him complaining that her ashes had been mislaid. Mollenhauer argued with the apparition, assuring his late mother that the arrangements had been properly made, but she showed him a little table with a wire basket, containing a small copper container.

The next morning Mollenhauer wanted to believe he dreamt the whole thing, but, nevertheless, he went to the cemetery and found that his mother's ashes were not where they were supposed to have been placed. They were found still in the undertaker's possession, exactly the way the late Mrs. Mollenhauer had shown them to her son! The ashes were properly placed and Bernard never heard from his mother again.

Thousands of such cases occur all over the world, suggesting they are not supernatural but merely extensions of human consciousness not yet fully understood.

Life magazine, in a recent survey entitled "A Crisis in Science," stated: "New enigmas in physics revive quests in metaphysics . . . the old-fashioned materialism is now even more old-fashioned . . . its basic assumption, that the only 'reality' is that which occupies space and has a mass, is irrelevant to an age that has proved that matter is interchangeable with energy . . . old-fashioned metaphysics, so far from being irrelevant to an age of science, is science's indispensable complement for a full view of life."

Dr. Gardner Murphy of the Menninger Foundation of Minnesota, and long-time president of the American Society for Psychical Research in New York, adds, "If there was one tenth of the evidence in any other field of science than there is in parapsychology, it would be accepted beyond question." Then: "There is more to man, more to him and his relationship with the cosmos than we have accepted. Further, this 'more' is of a different kind and order from the parts we know about," wrote Dr. Lawrence Le Shan, eminent researcher and author.

As we learn more about the nature of man, a breakthrough in our understanding of the elusive element of consciousness and its continuance beyond the physical body seems near. The very scientists who work in the most advanced physical sciences may well be the ones to furnish the final link.

Dr. Werner Schiebele, atomic physicist, stated in a lecture delivered at a conference on parapsychology in Constance, Germany: ". . . If during seances entities, phantoms, or spirits of the deceased appear which have been identified beyond the shadow of a doubt to be the people they pretend to be, they must be regarded as something more than the images of the dead. . . . Parapsychology has furnished definite proof for the continuance of life beyond physical death."

While I now regard Philip Solomon as the best medium in Great Britain, I feel the same about Yolana Lassaw in the U.S. I discovered her working as a housekeeper for a friend twenty-five years ago, and took a hand in training and steering her toward the mediumship which is her great gift. From time to time I visit her, and discuss possible television appearances and such with her. Invariably she will give me a spontaneous reading on the spot.

While much of this material pertains to predictions (most actually come true in her case), some have to do with contacts between discarnates from the Other Side and us. She does not go into deep trance when she does this, but is in a state of conscious relaxation as she repeats what she is being told or shown by the spirit communicators.

Only a week ago, my closest friend, Michael B., spoke through the medium. I demanded evidence that it was indeed he and she described him completely. But perfect evidence requires that something very specific and detailed be transmitted which is unknown to me and to the medium, the transmitter.

Within moments I received just that proof: A private matter regarding a temporary loan from mother to son, and the reasons for it, the name of that son, and other personal data (such as the maiden name of the son's wife) came through. None of these data were known to me nor were they accessible to the medium, some of it having just occurred, and none of it published, or public knowledge.

This then was the absolute proof Michael's widow had hoped for, and when I spoke to her later, she confirmed all the data received through Yolana as being correct.

Not every trance medium is as accurate or gifted as Yolana or Philip Solomon, but there must be others out there, unknown to me, who can also do this work. The Other Side and ours are always in contact, one way or another.

CHAPTER 2

PHILIP SOLOMON CONTACTS
HANS HOLZER

The July 1995 issue of *Fate* contained an article by me
about mediumship and how it should be evaluated; and in it I
wrote of the four leading American mediums I had tested and
found to be highly professional and evidential. The mediums
are: Yolana Lassaw, Rosanna Rogers, Marisa Anderson, and
Kathleen Karter. Apparently, the article so impressed British
medium Philip Solomon he decided to contact me, and, as my
address was listed at the end of the article, he was able to do so.

At this point Solomon knew nothing of me. The article
was the first piece of information regarding me and my work
that he had seen, and I, on the other hand, had not heard of
him and his work before either. But I was pleased with his
brief note of approval, and requested that he send me some
material about his work and past evidential credits. I suggested that if we ever met, I would want a sitting, as I always do
with new mediums, and he readily agreed.

But in this second letter, attached to the material about his
past record, were certain statements about me and my world
I found extremely interesting, seeing he knew nothing of my
family, my past, or details of my life; nor could he have read
of these in my books. He described me accurately as to habits,
feelings, and outlook, and stated that I became interested in

7

the psychic at age seven. This is exactly when it happened, due to the influence of a maternal uncle named Heinrich (Henry). In the same letter, he did a psychic reading for me spontaneously.

He mentioned a number of names of people on the Other Side who had a link to me and wanted to "get through" to me through his mediumship at that moment. These names were Eric, Peter, Martha, Rudi, Eddie, Alic, Alice, all of which made sense to me. He also hinted at some connection with the Russian czars, and wondered if it made any sense to me.

I confirmed the following with him on August 9, 1995: Eric was a close friend who died young in an industrial accident. Peter was a lifelong friend, though not close, who had died a few years ago. Martha is my late mother. Eddie was the husband of Alice, my aunt. Alic was my ex-wife's half-brother. The connection with the Russian czars is correct: my ex-wife Catherine was a direct descendant of Catherine the Great.

Considering that Philip Solomon could not possibly have access to these names and their connection with me, it is clear that the communications are genuine messages from the Other Side; nothing in the psychic field is without purpose, and the purpose here seems to be to acquaint me with the mediumship talents of a man I had never met.

Now it became a sort of routine that in the correspondence that ensued between us regarding his books and their feasibility for the American market, or the possibility of his coming to America for a working visit, there was often a "snippet," as Philip called it, of messages for me.

On September 1, 1995, he wrote: "Someone has a problem with their hands or hip . . . I get the names Nadine, Lisa, Marie, and Anna." My ex-mother-in-law was then suffering from problems in her wrists and hip, due to an old operation. Nadine is my daughter, thirty-five years old. Lisa was a close friend who died young. Marie and Anna were cooks in my grandmother's house and in my parents' house, and always cared for me.

On October 9, 1995, in response to my acknowledgement of these names, Philip wrote back, asking about Anna: "What's wrong with the grave?" I was shocked, because it happens that for a long time and after several attempts when in Austria, I could not locate her grave. Finally, in 1988, I found it, thanks to a cemetery employee who recognized the name.

As to the name Solomon, Philip disclosed that it is his pen name. The editor of a local newspaper for which he was then writing a column, decided to give it to him for obvious reasons: "Solomon the Wise." For the next two years or so, we had occasional contacts, mainly about his books and their possibilities over here and his possible visit. During that time Philip sent me predictions about my career and personal life, but by then he knew a good deal about both, so these "snippets," though amazingly accurate are not as astonishing as were the earlier ones when he knew nothing about my personal and professional life.

Of all the trance mediums today, I think Philip is the best in terms of giving names, situations, and details without having access to the people involved, nor any knowledge of books where such data might be found, because these data do not exist in published form, being strictly private matters. For example, only recently he brought through the brother of a friend, a brother who had passed over many years ago. He not only named him, but also described, accurately, physical marks like scars and where they were located; even though my friend had changed her name a long time ago. This of course was not known to the medium, nor to me at the time.

That, in fact, is the evidence that a spirit person is exactly what is claimed, a person alive and well in the next world with all memories and faculties intact.

All the beliefs and faith, all the conjectures, both religious and nonreligious, about the existence of another dimension beyond the physical world lack objective proof. What people like Philip Solomon do (and there are precious few like him) rely on none of the above. No alternate explanation can possibly explain the uncanny accuracy of specific information about someone's personal life when the medium has not met that person, nor knows anything about the person, and the recipient of those data (myself) is also unaware of all these matters, and the data are not public knowledge (as with some celebrities), nor are they to be found in any published record. This truly is absolute proof.

The will to disbelieve at all costs, displayed by professional skeptics to whom the notion of a realistic, verified spirit world is unacceptable, obscures the evidence for them. But to any rational and open-minded individual, no matter how cautious they might be in their acceptance, these data do suggest the validity of the evidence for the afterlife. Clearly, this is something of great concern to all who want contact with loved ones who have passed over. As such, it is an intensely personal matter.

By now, Philip's ability to do trance work and bring forth accurate contacts with the dead had so impressed me, it occurred to me that this material might make a useful book about the nature of the Other Side of life. Consequently, I proposed that he and I should collaborate on a book—this book—with the sole purpose of presenting detailed and specific information about life after death. Not the bits about "being so happy" over there, or religiously colored descriptions of Heaven, but information of the kind one obtains when travelling in a foreign or unknown country.

He readily agreed, and allowed regular trance sessions to take place during which all kind of spirits made contact—people he knew and many he did not, ordinary people as well as the famous. The material is presented here exactly as he received it. Because Philip was so obviously able to bring forth names and messages from people I knew in life, but to whom he had no access, it is fair to assume that the same authenticity prevails with his material involving others.

We should understand this: What Philip Solomon does is not to be confused with channeling as it is, alas, practiced in America, as a form of alleged communication with spirits, usually someone very famous or someone unknown you can't trace—contacts rarely, if ever, capable of true verification. Moreover, the material allegedly channeled from the Other Side is usually just pure philosophy rather than anything concrete. In my experience (and view), channeling and channelers belong to the realm of metaphysics relying on belief, not to the realm of paranormal experiences capable of proper scientific evaluation. There are a number of such channelers who pretend contact with a higher intelligence, when in fact it all comes from their own imagination, or, at best, from their unconscious.

But what Philip does is a form of trance mediumship, not channeling. "Channelling" accepts communications from parties unknown, never insisting on concrete identification of the source of communication. The people on the Other Side contact him whenever he makes himself available by "sitting" to receive their input, but he has no control whatever as to who and what will come through his mediumship, nor does he ever solicit anyone to make contact. However, in this experiment, and for our book, I instructed him to ask specific questions about the nature of the hereafter which resulted in specific data.

Those who have crossed over to the next dimension of life are no more or less human beings than they were before shedding their physical bodies. They are not wiser nor have they supernatural powers, and about the only thing they do possess now that they did not have before is direct knowledge of their own continuing existence and the world they live in. That knowledge is precisely what we have been after in this experiment.

When it comes to the persons thus communicating with the medium, there are three categories:

First, there are unknown people who use the opportunity to speak through a medium, chiefly to reach someone over here or to report about their own well-being. Second, there are people known to the medium, or people the medium knows are known to a client. Third, there are a sprinkling of so-called celebrities. To the critic, especially in the mainstream media, this smells of fakery, as so much is known about these people. But it is good copy to report such a contact and at the same time to sensationalize it, to ridicule the whole thing and cast doubt about the authenticity of the contact. But taken in the context of so many contacts, the material from celebrities

11

is no different than that from others and there is no reason to assume that celebrities, once over there, should not have the same desires or needs to communicate in this manner.

With that in mind, I present Philip's carefully recorded material, having not the slightest doubt regarding its authenticity and meaningful implications regarding a realistic survey of a dimension or a state of existence we all move into sooner or later. It still begs the question of God, or who instituted the system and when, but its very existence cannot be doubted from the mountains of evidence—not on a faith or belief basis.

As we get to understand what the afterlife really is like, it may well be that we gradually learn of the higher levels of consciousness and where they ultimately lead. But it also affects the way we live in the physical world. Clearly, none of our actions, especially violence or other misdeeds, are inconsequential when considered in the larger context of an afterlife, and, especially, after one becomes aware of the evidence for reincarnation. Ultimately, it is ourselves, our actions, which determine the further progress beyond physical death.

CHAPTER 3

INVESTIGATING THE OTHER SIDE

By the spring of 1998, Philip and I had agreed to do this book together. There were certain guidelines I felt were necessary to have an impact on open-minded, even skeptical, readers, because of the sheer volume of literature dealing with the subject.

On the one hand, there are volumes of metaphysical works not particularly concerned about objective proof in a scientific sense, where we are asked to take the word of the author for what he or she has experienced. On the other hand, mediumistic communications, when they are genuine and not fanciful "channeling," have always cast some light on elements of the afterlife, nearly always in a positive manner. I don't recall a single instance of communications from "hell." There is a certain difficulty in separating established and ingrained religious beliefs of the afterlife from the facts as borne out by the evidence, but that is very necessary if one is searching for objective truth, and not belief.

What I wanted Philip to go after was detailed and specific information, descriptions of a typical "day in the afterlife" of the communicator, whoever that might turn out to be. Celebrities were not excluded provided they were part of the overall number of communicators, not specifically sought out in any way. But Philip assured me he did not ever seek out anyone over there, that it was always the other way around, as it should be. Notwithstanding the fact that people do naturally reach out to their loved ones in times of stress of one kind or another, the response, that is the actual contact, depends on permission for it from the guide on the Other Side before it occurs.

During the summer months of 1998, Philip held regular trance sessions allowing communicators to use his mediumship to come through with information regarding their condition, activities, and the nature of the Other Side in terms of their own existence. During that time, nearly every communication from Philip contained bits and pieces of personal messages for me, always with a name attached, quite specific, and whose meaning I was able to understand as to my ongoing life.

When the material Philip wrote was in my hands, I was satisfied it represented perhaps the first real account of the afterlife in specific and non-glamorous, non-religious terms, as if the communicator over there had simply moved to a "foreign country" and was reporting what it was like in every department of life.

Philip did not "call on" any of the spirit communicators; all he did was make himself available. To be sure, Philip did not address anyone specific in the world of spirit, but allowed himself to be contacted by anyone who wished to do so. Clearly, our intention of collaborating on a book specifically dealing with actual and detailed conditions about the next level of existence must have been known to the guides there to make this possible, which convinces me that this project has the support of the guides (the officials in charge of communication, to be exact), otherwise it surely would not have occurred.

No attempt is made here to verify if individuals unknown to Philip actually existed; that was not the issue, as we were not dealing with their earthly life at all. They might bring that themselves if it was their wish and had some significance in the account they were giving, but Philip took them at their word, because, after all, it was their account we wanted to have and nothing more.

The communications often are questions and answers between Philip and the discarnates, in which he wants to get more specific data about their lives. But these questions are the kind an investigative reporter would ask the subject of his interview, and that was precisely what I instructed the medium to do. After all, those who live on the Other Side have retained their character, personality, and abilities to respond, and the only way for us to access real information about their existence there was to look at it from our point of view, since it is meant for those on *this* side of life who wish to know more about theirs. These protocols, as they were, will be given verbatim further on, without any editing on my part.

Finally, in the matter of celebrities or well-known persons of whom much is generally known or easily accessible, why should they not also wish to communicate? This is not a book proving the afterlife. First, it requires no additional proof, and second, the very nature of these communications adds to the body of proof that is already staggering. Our sole purpose is to be more detailed and specific about the world beyond, as understood from our point of view, than other accounts have been. By doing so, a great deal of traditional ideas about Heaven and Hell will vanish for most of our readers, and some die-hard fundamentalists may even take offense at hearing our report. Truth is never pleasing to everybody, at least not at first. But eventually, it does prevail.

The very best mediums can establish proof of contact with a discarnate, a spirit person, by mentioning the name and sometimes a message for the client. Sometimes they can only describe the spirit person and the client recognizes that person. But I have never met any professional medium who can rattle off a dozen names and their particular relationship to the client or recipient the way Philip does repeatedly. For a dear friend of mine, whom Philip knew nothing of but her first name, and whom he had never met, he produced the name of her son, that he had committed suicide, and that in life he had taken care of his brother's children! He then proceeded to name four of her close business associates with whom she was dealing at this time.

In a communication from Philip of November 11, 1998, he stated that my loved ones were concerned about my health. I had fallen just two weeks prior! Philip mentioned my father, Leo; my uncle Heinrich; a nurse-like governess; and the names Fritz and Tony. I immediately asked for the nurse-governess' name, and without hesitation he replied, "Anna," which was correct. Yet he and I had never even met! Fritz was an old school chum, and Tony is someone I am currently working with on a musical project.

These kinds of specifics are rare. I am mentioning this because what follows are communications from spirits I don't know, and, in many cases, Philip does not know either. To prove their existence would not be difficult, but time consuming, and as the thrust of this work is not proving the individual survival of otherwise average people, but their account of the afterlife as seen through their eyes, I did not want to hold up this project for a considerable period just because of that.

I asked Philip to describe the mechanics, the conditions of his contacts with those living on the Other Side.

"It is always they who contact me," he explained, "usually at a quiet time when I am relaxed, but it can be at any time. At other times, I will deliberately sit and say a prayer followed by invoking psychic protection, and ask if anyone wishes to pass messages over. I can work in ordinary everyday consciousness or in deep trance. It is not a structured condition. When I am working for people, I like to get a written letter and sometimes their date of birth to start the link. Of course, to speak over the phone is better, one-to-one in person even more so.

"I have seen spirit people all my life. I remember having quite a long chat with my late grandmother when I was about three. Sometimes I see those with messages, but more often I just hear the voice, a bit like a telephone switchboard operator. It is hectic at times, especially when I am on stage. I have had them lining up to communicate with their loved ones in the audience, and at times they are impatient and insistent. When they visit they are usually the same as when they were in the body, but sometimes there is a cool or warm feeling, and sometimes I smell something like lavender or roses."

Philip Solomon demonstrates his gift as a natural medium, and he does it well. The proof of the pudding, so to speak, is in the results: information of a detailed and specific nature he could not possibly have known or had access to in any way whatever, and which turns out to be correct. Here is what he says on this:

"Does the spirit world exist? Yes, I would claim, as would any other genuine medium. Yet in truth we never really can give the positive, physical evidence that would prove its existence. For the human mind cannot comprehend or communicate with a source of power that is beyond its understanding or comprehension. How do you explain to someone born deaf the beauty of the spoken word or the music of the maestro? You cannot, although with a little training the vibration of such lovely things can be felt and sensed. In truth, none of us will know for sure if the spirit world exists until we pass away.

"There is not, and will not be a complete physical demonstration or proof to be had for those we understand as having 'passed away,' but the evidence is certainly there for two worlds if only you will see and feel it and nurture its beautiful vibration. We know for sure our world exists, yet are only beginning to understand its physics and the way it functions in our galaxy. Yet many of the scientists who have only just come to grips with its complexity would arrogantly and foolishly tell you the spirit world does not exist because they do not understand it. What pompous and arrogant fools they are!

"Communication with people like you and me who live in the spirit world is made possible by mediums living in our physical world who have the gifts called clairvoyance, clairaudience, and clairsentience. Clairvoyant people see the spirit world. I have had this gift since I was a little boy and without it could not hope to explain spirit matters in this book, which my friend Hans Holzer and I have put together. Clairaudient people hear the spirit world but don't see it, and simply pass on the messages between the two worlds. Clairsentient people smell the fragrances and sweet perfumes that abound in the spirit realms, and this ability is often the first gift of a developing medium. There are also some mediums who communicate by writing or drawing pictures, making beautiful portraits of those in the spirit realms. The British psychic Coral Polge is a very good example of one who does this type of work. Some mediums work as the specific channel of individuals in the spirit world. The London housewife Rosemary Brown has received communications from some of the great composers in history including Franz Liszt, whom Rosemary claims to have known from her childhood; she also received messages from Beethoven and Chopin. Rosemary had very little professional training in music, yet professional musicians in both America and Great Britain have claimed that her work is of a very, very high standard and very similar to the individual works of the great composers.

"Many mediums also make predictions, and I have done this type of work, though this is certainly not new. In the past, many things have been predicted that have come to pass, and, as an example, both in England and America, many mediums and psychics had predicted the downfall of the unfortunate Titanic.

"I have put together a few examples of the connections that are made between this world and the spirit world hoping to convince you, the reader, of the possibilities. I would at least ask you to be open-minded and read our book in this context. Of course there are those who will say everything I have told you is false or is from my imagination, and who am I to argue with them? I shall never convince them, so I find solace in the words of the immortal Oscar Wilde who said, 'where ignorance is bliss, 'tis folly to be wise.'"

Here, then, are Philip Solomon's verbatim accounts of his discussions, in an appropriate trance state, with those living on the Other Side of Life as recorded by him.

CHAPTER 4

DAVID'S PROGRESSION
TO THE HIGHER LIFE

This information was given to me, Philip Solomon, clairaudiently by David on February 28, 1998. David was born and lived in Camden Town, London, and worked from the 1930s to 1950s as a tailor.

"Philip, when we come to the end of our time in our physical life, all of us, whatever our background, make the move onto another level of existence, and this is a transfer from a physical being to a spirit being. In truth, I tell you, very little changes; the personality, likes and dislikes, memories, and the love of spiritual and, indeed, physical things, remains. I have to be honest and tell you something that often disappoints a lot of my closest friends. The hard-hearted businessman or woman does not suddenly become a loving, caring, progressed soul just because they have now moved into the spirit world! Our progression and the learning of wisdom and the understanding of higher things have to be earned, but, undoubtedly, when we reach that stage, all of us have made an upward start at least.

"Also be assured that it is still quite possible for us to take shape and form; have the vision to see and the senses to love, care, touch and feel; and to have the pleasure and contentment of our own personal home or place to stay and to be part of happy, reunited family groups; to be, basically, around those we love and who will love us in a happy and contented home. Of course, these are things that would make us happy in the physical body, and as I have already told you, we do not really change, so they also make us happy in the spirit world. Those in the spirit world are always keen to communicate with their loved ones in this existence and, indeed, with others who are of interest to them in your world; although, in general terms, this has to be through the art of mediumship. All of us will sense or be aware of our loved ones around us at some time or another. This is especially so in times of need or perhaps when you think to yourself, 'If only I could get some guidance,' and then suddenly you get the answer in your head, and although it is easy to think it is just a coincidence, believe me it is not.

"There are many, unfortunately, who do not believe in an afterlife, but they will also have kind, loving spirit people who will always be there trying to help them as best they can. At death, the time they will see as their darkest moment, they will still see a wonderful light as a loving partner, mother, father, or other dear friend who walks forth and offers to take them to the Other Side. At this moment, it matters not whether you are a believer, non-believer, devout spiritualist, religious, or atheist. Loved ones are there for you always.

"Sometimes people are moved over unexpectedly before their time, as in the awful situation of a road accident, or from being violently murdered, or by the very sad act of suicide. There are colleagues and mediums in your world who say that these people have great difficulty in transferring to the higher life, and, especially in the cases of suicide, they do not immediately enter the spirit realms. What utter rot! Do not agree with them. It may well be that they are sick and very tired by their physical conditions, but from the moment they reach the spirit world, healing and mending are in place for them by excellent doctors, physicians, and nurses, who often continue the calling they had in their physical life. Most importantly, these new entrants to the spirit realms are cared for by their relatives, loved ones, and friends.

"But let me go on and explain the normal, everyday existence people have with all their normal faculties after they step through the veil of death. In the spirit world the individual being will still be aware that he or she has a viewable body and that he can walk, talk, and communicate with others; that he is an entity who still has control over himself; that his own personality and intelligence are still present. As he meets other loved ones who have progressed to the spirit world he will see that they too possess form, that their personalities are still in place, and that they have simply entered a different kind of body than their previous physical one. As he hugs and greets his friends there is a feeling of merging and love he would never have sensed or felt in a physical way."

These words tell how David described his progression in the spirit world as he was reunited with his beloved wife. He says he was surprised to find he was not at all tired, and although in his late seventies in a physical way, he felt the fitness and energy levels he had when he was perhaps twenty-seven. There was so much to see and be aware of, he did feel a little overwhelmed. Susan, his wife, held out her hand and called him forward.

"Where will we go?" asked David.

She smiled and laughed the way she did when she was a young girl. "I am taking you to a place I have prepared for you, David."

In a matter of seconds they arrived at a beautiful bungalow, strangely, the type of home he had always wished to live in when he was in the body but had never actually owned.

Once inside the building, David saw in front of him a tall, handsome, glowing man with the most beautiful blue eyes he had ever seen in his life. David knew this was someone very special to him and that he was a very kind man.

"Are you the Master, Our Lord?" asked David.

"No, no," laughed the man. "But I am the friend who has been with you from the very moment you chose to be born. I was always there at your shoulder."

"Like my guardian angel?" asked David.

"Yes," said the man. "In some ways that is a good

explanation. but I would describe myself as a teacher, a person who chose to help you. Indeed, I chose to work with you, and in time, David, you may wish to do likewise with someone who is in the living body. For now, David, go on into that room there." The man motioned and pointed to a room at the side.

David did so, and before him in the room stood all his loved ones who had passed over some years before. In a strange awareness, all the little things he had liked in his physical life also seemed to be there in that tiny room—the rabbit he had kept as a pet when he was a little boy, his favorite books, a favorite pair of slippers, and much more. There also stood his mother, Sarah, and immediately David was overcome with emotion and started to cry, "Mum, mum, I love you."

"And I love you too, son," she replied.

His father, Tom, grabbed his hands and shook them. "Son, it is so good to see you. I am so very proud of all the things you have achieved."

David shook his head in wonder and hugged them both.

"Look over there," said his mother, and pointed to the most beautiful girl he had ever seen. "That is your sister, Elizabeth Jane."

"But mum, I didn't have a sister, did I?"

His mother beamed and reminded him of the time when he was about three years old and she had told him she had lost a baby. "This is your sister from that time. She has always been close to you and has grown to great beauty in the spirit world. Your father and I are so proud of her for she does so much work for spirit and chooses to help those still in the body."

David and his sister held each other close as though they had known each other forever, and I suppose in truth they had.

All around David stood aunts and uncles, cousins and friends, and those he had thought were lost to him; but now they stood before him clearly showing they loved him and were welcoming him home. The man who had greeted David then suggested to everyone it would be nice if they left David and Susan alone for a while so they could spend time together and so David could come to terms with the changes to his existence. The man David had perceived to be his guardian angel then placed David's hand in his wife's, Susan's, and ushered his loved ones away and closed the door to the bungalow behind him leaving David in blissful happiness.

David loved the home Susan had made for them. It was very different from the house they had shared in London, which had been a very small terraced house in row after row of other similar buildings. In their spirit home, there was a lot of space and everything was new, and sparkled in beautiful colors, some not known or seen in the physical world. Wonderful plants, trees, and flowers grew all around them. Other dwellings nearby were occupied by friends and loved ones, but there was enough space between each house to allow privacy and proper contemplation of their own thoughts. This was something that both David and Susan had longed for in their physical life in London; it was now theirs in the Higher Life.

Around Susan's home there was no bad weather or the awful smog that had covered most of London in the 1930s. Here, the home had skylights that looked to the stars, yet rain never fell; this was a place free of such earthly things. Susan asked David to remove his clothes and smiled shyly. He looked surprised, but did so, and immediately noticed how young and firmly muscled his body had become, more like when he had been twenty-four than the earthly body he had just left behind, riddled with arthritis and illnesses. Susan removed her robe revealing that she also had a form and shape similar to when she was a young woman. Joining hands they blended in a most beautiful way.

After a while Susan told David to take away his old clothes, which were crumpled in a heap, and to throw them outside. As he did so they seemed to dissolve before his eyes. She then told him to pick up the radiant spiritual gown and at once he felt in perfect balance with it. For a time Susan and David sat and experienced the joy of being together again after so long, and they were wholeheartedly content in their reunion.

David, suddenly looking serious, asked Susan why she had not come for him sooner. "Did you not know how much I loved you and how desperately sad and lonely I was without you?"

Susan gazed deeply into his eyes and replied, "David, I was always right there with you. So were your mother and sister, especially in your most lonely and sad times. You will never know how much I missed not having you with me, or how much I cared, but it had to be. We just could not be together at that time. But now we are together and you and I will keep this love forever, and as best we can we will help those in the other world to get by, especially when they are sad and lonely. I tell you in truth now, David, they will feel the same about you as you did about me, and they will be so aware of their own grief they will not be aware of our presence. If only those in the body could realize this truth and the feelings that could be expressed between us in the two worlds; but it is the most difficult and complex of situations to understand and accept, and again, in truth, it is only understood by the majority of people when they come and join us in the spirit world."

They sat a little longer and talked of their memories and how glad they were to be together again; then Susan turned to him and said, "But David, you won't always want to be with me just sitting at my side holding my hand."

"I never want to be apart from you again!" exclaimed David.

"Hush, hush, and listen to what I tell you," answered his wife gently. "After a short period you must learn to progress as an individual. Just as you did in the physical world, so you must progress here in the spirit world. Soon you will want to learn everything about this place and you will want to see in what ways you can help those who are left behind in the physical world as well. What you have seen so far in this short period of existence here is but a tiny glimpse of wonders totally beyond your comprehension."

As Susan looked at her husband she realized he was now getting a little confused with all the information she was giving him and said, "Never mind darling, for now we are eternally reunited. Come and relax in my home . . . Susan's home . . . Susan and David's home!"

David finished this communication by saying, "This is my experience of the spirit world, Philip, I hope it is helpful to your work."

CHAPTER 5

PATRICK'S STORY

Patrick O'Kelly communicated with me on March 4, 1998 in the early hours of the day, apparently aware of the book Hans and I were writing. This is the story of his life on the Earth plane and his experiences of the spirit world. In the body, Patrick had lived a severe life, blazing drunk most of the time. He claims he lived in Ireland in the early 1890s. It would seem he had a reasonable start in life, although I am not sure that is true.

Patrick told me he inherited and took over the business of his father's Irish jaunting car, which was apparently a type of taxi service. Basically, it was a small two-wheeled carriage pulled by a good horse. When sober, he operated a good service around the O'Connell Bridge area of Dublin. Patrick also seemed to have a terrible hatred of the British, calling them the "Devil's own people," and blaming them for just about everything that went wrong in his life, including the death of his wife, Kitty, who died in childbirth with their sixth child. Kitty also had a terrible problem with drinking. After the loss of his wife, Patrick made his way to New York, without a ticket, on what he called the "big ships" that were docked nearby. Then, apparently, within weeks he lost his life in a fistfight with another Irishman. Patrick spoke very little of love in his early years of childhood and it would appear to me from some of the things he said he had been an orphan rather than the son of a rich man, though he never confirmed any of these things to me. When I asked him these questions I didn't get any response.

By the age of twenty, Patrick was married, and by twenty-six, he and his wife Kitty had five children. To use his words, the only things that brought real love into his life "was the poteen and the porter," apparently drinks that were favorites among the lower classes of the Irish at this time. By the age of thirty-two, Patrick's life was finished and he moved onto his place in the spirit world.

I think one of the very important things about Patrick's story, despite the awful experiences he suffered in his life, was that there were lessons for him to learn. It is amazing how very different is his view of the spirit world. When Patrick arrived in the spirit world, he found Kitty and other relatives waiting for him. Strangely, he had been taken up by his father, Michael, a man whom he had not been close to and had feared; yet, in his words, he was the only one able to convince Patrick that he was dead or had left his earthly body behind.

After his reunion with Kitty, Patrick often let the memories of his earthly life come to mind, and he would go back in time and think of the life he had spent and would see himself and his family in all the awful times they had endured—which was the complete opposite of the lovely place, of gifts, and of things that were being given to him now. But Patrick needed some time to rehabilitate, and this was a place very much like a hospital, but with no painful surgery or tests; only the sounds and beautiful colors that seemed to flood his body and mind and make him feel very good within himself, vibrant and in perfect health.

He spoke of the very wise men and women who told him during this period of rehabilitation why he had suffered in his life. They told him that later in his progression there would come a day when he would join them, helping others get through difficult times in their life so they could progress. Patrick was particularly keen to impress upon me that it didn't matter how you were or what sort of condition you were in when you passed over; no matter how ill you were, that you would immediately be put right. In this particular communication, he specifically wanted to talk to me about a place he called the "healing houses," and this is what he had to say:

"The healing houses are for people newly arrived in the spirit world and are beautiful buildings as you will see when your time comes and the guides take you there. Just by spending time there you are brought into perfect health. We do not have illnesses and conditions like you do in the physical body. Sometimes, while healing is taking place in these places, it is hard for the individual to communicate with the living, basically because they are still weak. Many times our loved ones will think that because someone has passed over and they do not get through to them through a medium, or something similar, immediately, they do not care, but this is not the case at all. It is just a matter of spending time to recuperate and get themselves fit.

"You must remember that time is very different in the spirit world from what it is on Earth. There are not the same rushed times and deadlines to be met; therefore, it may be that the patient may stay in these healing houses for several years until they feel they are perfectly ready to progress on to doing other things. Some spirit beings choose to help others, not just their loved ones within their family groups."

Indeed, Patrick has now taken on this role and he has evolved to the stage where he often uses his experiences from when he was in the physical body to help those who are suffering from things such as alcohol abuse, terrible childhood experiences, or, basically, lacking enough things to get by. Although we are often not aware of it in the physical body, the spirit world is always trying to help poor souls such as these to progress, and perhaps unless you actually experience these awful things in life the way Patrick did now, could you progress, and when you join spirit, have the wish, knowledge, and ability to come back and help those who are suffering similarly.

There were many important issues that Patrick specifically wanted to get through for this book. One is that no matter how ill or troubled you are, the minute you go into the spirit world, healing begins to take place. Another is that if you have suffered in this life then there is a meaning for it and some good always comes out of it. In Patrick's case, it has given him the knowledge and the wisdom from the spirit world to help others.

CHAPTER 6

THE WORDS OF FATHER THOMAS

This communication comes from Father Thomas, March 7, 1998, at 9:45 P.M.:

"The spirit world is so different from yours and is beyond your comprehension, my friend. Blessed as you are you cannot know its wisdom until you join us here and take your place working alongside us. There is no illness or pain, except when you first come over, but all is quickly put in balance in readjustment centers. These are what you might see as hospitals, but they are more to do with vibration fields and colors which harmonize, attune, and balance the spirit. There is no sex between spirit beings but many do choose to blend. By this I mean perfect telepathic communication to achieve a state of pure love. Neither do we reject those of unclear gender; all are part of one unequivocal Love. We do not work for money or reward as people would, Philip, on the Earth plane, and yet if you enjoyed that occupation it could be available to you here. If the carpenter needs wood, wood is provided. If the physician or nurse still needs to practice, then a surgery is there. In truth, Philip, you can do anything that pleases and progresses you, for almost all want to progress and learn. This is done by study under one of the great teachers and their helpers.

"Many people in your world speak of guides working with and through them, but I tell you in truth, Philip, this is not a common happening. The guides, as you call them, are here teaching many others, those who have made their progression from your world and who wish to go back and help others, to have the knowledge and ability to do so. There are colors and hues that you will never see outside the spirit world, and on this plane we have many lovely places to visit of indescribable beauty. It is so easy to get to these places when in spirit as the merest thought of them and you are there. Indeed, when we so wish to use our thoughts in this way we can be anywhere we wish, including your plane. This is the way spirit entities visit your plane. You should never doubt our presence for we are often with you and those with the perception of clairvoyance see us clearly.

"It is difficult for you to understand the spirit world, I know, but if you can imagine a place where anything and everything is available to you, this is it. Those who are tone deaf but love music not only listen but play instruments and play beautiful music themselves. Those who admire paintings and drawings still do so but also paint and draw them for themselves as they sit alongside the masters they so admire. Those who have worked for spirit now join their former teachers and teach others and help those in your world. Those who have been unloved are loved. The blind see and the deaf hear. All that you want is given here. You simply think of it and it is there, and when it is no longer desired, it dissolves away.

"Many in your world worry when a loved one comes to us and they are left behind that if they remarry or relove, who will they be with when they come to us. This is very amusing to us for its answer is so very simple: When you come to us you will simply think where you want to be or whom you wish to be with and there you will be. Nothing could be more simple. It is simply your first thought away. There is no violence, greed, or jealousy in the spirit world. Once you pass through the healing sanctuaries, all these things are over and left behind; yet sometimes when an entity being wishes to keep these vices, a move over takes a little longer, but in the end all do come to us. For instance, it is a foolish thing to say that those who take their own lives do not come to us. They do, all of them, but those who are in your world should know that if you commit this act, suicide, with the wish to be with someone you love, then it will take a much longer time for you to reach them, for a much longer time will be spent in the healing sanctuaries. This can, at times, be the same situation for those who have passed over before their time through accidents or the awful act of murder, although these people will always have the support and helping guidance of their loved ones. All things in progression have to be earned.

"I have tried very hard, Philip, in a few simple words to explain to you what the spirit world is like so that you and your good friend, Hans, can tell the way things are for us in this existence. Always be assured the spirit world is God's gift to all. Thank you."

CHAPTER 7

AN INTERVIEW WITH THE KING, ELVIS

This communication came from Elvis Presley on March 17, 1998, at 7:15 P.M.:

"I'm real pleased you and Mr. Holzer are gettin' this book together. Too many folks get a real misunderstanding about what it's like over here. Yes sir, when I was living I always thought about things, maybe the same way you do, y'know, that there'd be angels, Heaven in the sky, and Jesus. But man, these sort of things are way above what's on this second level I've come to!"

"So there are other levels then?" I asked.

"Sure! Lots of them. When I was in your world I met lots of them famous psychics who all said they had guides that were hundreds, maybe thousands of years old. Maybe some of them did, but I tell you, sir, most of those old ones are from much higher levels and wouldn't spend too much time wanting to speak with folks, even mediums, on the Earth plane."

"So it's their imagination then?" I asked. "Or they make it up? Elvis, these people they are supposed to talk to—Indian chiefs and ancient kings and queens—they're not their personal guides on Earth then?"

"Well, yes sir, like I said, most of these people imagine these things, but not always. Maybe some of them do get messages and advice from these higher teachers, but usually it's from people like me and others who have passed over quite recently and, you know, wanna come back sometimes and help folks get along a little better! And if you were lucky enough to be famous like me, you can teach people to live good, clean lives away from drugs and crime."

I asked, "Elvis, is that what you are telling people, not to have anything to do with crime and drugs?"

"Yes sir, that's exactly what I'm coming through to tell you today to tell people, and I have been getting this through to Mr. Holzer for many years."

"Can you tell me what it's specifically like in the spirit world, Mr. Presley?"

"Call me 'Elvis,' or 'E,' man!"

"Okay, Elvis, what's it like then?"

"Just like in the good old U.S. of A., man! Everything I ever wanted when I was really, really happy, I've got here! I always liked people around me who I knew cared for me and here I've got my momma, Daddy, the Dodger, Rozella, Grandma Doll, and Grandpa Jessie, my twin brother Jessie, and Morning Dove and Grandpa Billie. I like to spend a lot of time around them. Them and Momma are helping me a lot right now."

"So you spend a lot of time with your family then?"

"Sure, wouldn't you?"

"Yes, I suppose I would. Do you still entertain, Elvis?"

"I was born in your world and reborn in spirit to entertain. Of course I do! But my shows now are bigger and better and are like big spirituals—gatherings if you like. You know, that's always something I wanted to do in the body but the Colonel never really let me get the chance to do it. Money, money, money—that's all he ever wanted. Still, I suppose that was his job, and he must have loved it, the old son of a bitch! In his thinking, he's still my manager here you know! Well, like I say, it's about being personally happy over here and it sure seems to make him happy and it's sure good to see his wife so well. She's a real nice lady and had a lot of suffering in her body, you know, when she was in your world."

"Elvis, you still haven't told me what you do."

34

"Oh yeah, okay. Well, I get up late, never before midday, and I make a little bit of music with a few close friends, like Roy Orbison, Buddy Holly, Beethoven—no, I'm joking with you. I'll be serious. I do play my music, and I sure do still like to entertain my fans with concerts and what have you, just the same as when I was in the body. But I am also doing a lot of work to inspire people like you, Philip, and Hans, to help others live better lives on the Earth plane."

"You know, sometimes, Elvis, it seems to me you weren't very happy when you were in the body."

"No man, I don't complain about those things; I got what I deserved. If you take every young girl that comes your way and hog out on cheeseburgers, fried peanut butter sandwiches, and just about any drug you can get some poor doctor to prescribe, you get what you deserve, 'cos for sure I got exploited by a lot of people. Perhaps no American ever got more exploited!"

"Do you miss people from down here?"

"No man. Like I say, you are still aware of them and come close when you want to."

"But physically?"

"Yeah, I suppose I miss my little cousin Billy Smith and, you know, Philip, perhaps I didn't realize it in the body, but Linda Thompson and Ann Margaret were real good friends to me and, of course, Lisa Marie and the little ones are very important to me. Yeah, maybe even Priscilla, too. She was the mother of my child, wasn't she? Trouble was, we were just too much like each other and you can make of that what you like, but that was the truth and very few people knew that. Anyway, Philip, I'm afraid that's it, I've got some work to do."

"What do you mean work?"

"How many times do I have to tell you? Things are whatever we want them to be over here. I'm going to play some spiritual music and it's on tour with a few of the boys."

Elvis laughed, then everything went silent. The communication was over.

CHAPTER 8

INTERVIEW WITH DR. ROBERTS

This communication was with Dr. Roberts on March 20, 1998, at 9:25 A.M. Dr. Roberts, in the body, lived and practiced in a South Wales mining community. Basically, in this communication I asked Dr. Roberts exactly what his life was like in spirit, asking him to perhaps describe the things he had done in the body. Dr. Roberts pointed out that spiritualists and others who claim to know what-is-what claim the spirit world is a dimension that constantly penetrates our own and that a reattunement of vibrations is all that is basically required to see what we would call the dead. But without great efforts we cannot see them and they cannot see us. I asked Dr. Roberts to describe the afterlife.

"When it comes your time to die, our first job over here is to convince you exactly what has happened to you, although you will have an immediate conscious understanding to some degree. The place you enter after death is relevant to the type of life you have lived as a physical being, and the place you live in and sense around you will very much be to your mental wishes of what you want them to be. Always be good and generous in the body and a more beautiful a place will await you in the spirit world, or Heaven, if you prefer."

"Can you give me an example, Dr. Roberts?" I asked.

"That is difficult, but I will try. Have you read of the great work of Sister Dora, who did wonderful nursing work in the area of the English Midlands of where you live?"

"Yes, of course I have. There is a statue of her in Walsall, which is very close to my home," I answered.

"Then you will appreciate that when the good Sister came to us it was quite natural that a wonderful hospital would be there for her and that work and a role would be provided for her where she could accommodate and work with those who have passed to the higher life quite recently. So, she continued her wonderful healing work. It is natural for you on the Earth plane to worry about death. We understand that, but the minute it happens, you enter a wonderful world where anything is possible, where you can do or be or achieve anything you want, and anything, even communication with those whom you wish to speak with is only a thought away.

"Let me make it very simple for you, Philip. When you come to us, your thoughts fit and create an environment very similar to the one on Earth, only with all the good things you enjoy and which will make you blissfully happy. The places you see and the people who are here are real, for they also bring with them into the spirit world their memories and expectations. Basically, in the spirit world, when you think something, it immediately becomes a reality. As you come up to this existence you mold and create everything around you. Memories and hoped-for dreams therefore become practical reality."

I asked Dr. Roberts what happened to disabled people, such as someone who has had to spend most of their life without an arm or a leg. "Is it true that at the moment of progression to the higher life, as almost all teachers tell us, the body becomes complete? What is the truth?"

"Philip, for someone with your higher spiritual intelligence, I am beginning to lose patience with you. Have I not told you that in this afterlife you can be anywhere or anyone you wish to be, whole or part? If you want to show yourself to loved ones, or perhaps to a medium to prove your existence, with the disability, or the missing arm, as you put it, then you think it and be it. Equally, if you wish to have the mind of a genius and the body of an athlete that would also be there for you. With the method of communication available to us I cannot make that any clearer."

I then asked Dr. Roberts a question I am sure many others have asked before. "How does everyone exist there? Surely with the millions of people going there over the years, it must be a very crowded place."

The doctor laughed but then continued with this answer: "This world we are talking about, Philip, is just the start of a long journey. There are many other levels and higher dimensions to progress to. Shortly after death, the spirit sometimes stays very close to Earth, for a little while, in what could be described as a transitional period of physical to spirit; and even this is another level of existence beyond your understanding. But it is very relevant to love and wish to remain with those left behind, while memories of your physical existence, pleasures, and all such things, are still very strong for you."

I asked Dr. Roberts how many levels there were. "This is not quite so simple to explain as you would request, for there are many altering states that you would not understand at this stage; but in very basic terms there are seven levels. The first is the one I explained to you; it is very close to the physical, Earth body that you operate in when you first leave the physical. The seventh level which is the highest is a very spiritual realm. This is where the great teachers, prophets, and wise ones gather alongside angels and the Godhead itself. In your physical life, there is often a term used in your very happiest moments, that you are 'in Seventh Heaven.' Such is this place—perfection on the seventh level. Many people who have lived very good lives on Earth feel they will come straight to this level, but that is not so, and most people actually go to the second level and enjoy materialist visions and experiences that they would have wished for in their Earth body. Even this constitutes a very difficult lesson, giving up physical pleasures. In time, those who learn the most wisdom progress to higher levels of existence."

"What about those who have been wicked in this life, who have committed murders and awful crimes? Do they go to the same lovely places that you described, those places that we wish for our parents, partners, and loved ones?"

"Philip, every single being in your world has a place prepared for them here in the spirit world. Even those who are bad and evil must be given the opportunity to progress and repent. The Hell you speak of in your existence is not really known to us. In truth, you will surely create your own Hell. For example, the wealthy, greedy businessman who adored his Cadillac more than his grandchildren will first visualize that same material thing when he comes to this world. But with learning and progression, advancement is there for all."

I had to tell Dr. Roberts I was still very confused about these levels and what the spirit world was like. Could he explain them in more detail to me? He agreed to explain the type of things that would happen to us, and what the different levels were.

"Level one is the place many have spoken of as Hell, Purgatory, and other such religious terms, but that is not what it is in truth. As I have told you, many people who have not lived good lives or have lived very bad lives will come to this place, and knowledge and understanding will be put there for them to help them come to understand their mistakes and misunderstandings so they may progress to a higher level. Strong influence is kept over this place so that those who have offended against mankind, and those you would describe as evil spirits and evil entities, who would try to badly influence those of your plane are severely restricted. It is an unfortunate fact, Philip, that there are many in your world who try to communicate with the spirit realms without the appropriate training or experience often using Ouija boards or other such equipment. They make contact with those who would scare or badly influence you from this level, very near to the physical sphere that I shall call level one.

"Most people quickly pass through or around this level and enter into what we call the second level of existence. This is very much a transitional place where we have healing sanctuaries and hospitals for those who have newly passed on to higher levels to alter and heal themselves. I spoke to you earlier in this communication about your ability to visualize, perceive, and experience bliss in the spirit realms, and it is often said you speak of Heaven upon Earth when you are very happy. That would be a very good description of this level for this really would be so. Communication is allowed between loved ones in your world and in our world, and it comes from this level, but you should remember it comes from very early days in their progression. This is why, sometimes, very genuine mediums are seen as charlatans or frauds when they are perfectly honest individuals. Communication between your world and this level of existence can often be misinterpreted by the best of mediums. Very few can link up like you, Philip.

"The third level for you as you make your progression is a wonderful place. This is the place that would be known in religious quarters as paradise, nirvana, and other such descriptions of wonderment beyond your understanding at the moment. Some who have lived wonderful lives on your plane or who have inspired others sometimes come straight to this level after their passing. There are people you have known in your life, who you loved and cared for, who are here. It is not necessary for me to name them for you to know them, for such wonderful people amongst you make this progression from their work.

"However, generally almost everyone has to spend time in realm two, reflecting on their life and how they spent it for the good or otherwise, contemplating the lessons they did or did not learn. It is from this level those who wish to return to your Earth plane are given that opportunity to relearn and progress; but I promise you, Philip, that the decision to come back and learn again is made by the individual and is not taken lightly. I am sure you and your friends understand that progression to a higher spiritual level is very attractive at this stage. This is also the place from which real messages for world change and improvements are channeled to the mediums in your world. This is a place of dual inspiration for the individual and the world.

"Progression to the fourth level, Philip, is a massive move forward. Material things are of no importance whatsoever, and often on this level of existence groups of spirits combine to influence and bring change, knowledge, and understanding to those in the levels below them. Perhaps almost equally important to the Earth realm, they inspire wonderful inventions, medical cures, and, perhaps most importantly, spiritual knowledge to those on your plane, often inspiring those who speak of peace and love in your world. This inspiration of course is often from those who have spent time on your Earth plane and, although they have made that progression to the fourth level, they still care and wish to help you in your existence. When people speak of great spirit guides such as Indian chiefs, wise men, learned monks, and clergy, who overshadow and communicate with mediums, this is the place from which that knowledge is transferred to your Earth plane.

"To progress to the fifth level is exceedingly hard, and in truth I say to you, Philip, although I will explain it in the best way you can understand, it is beyond your comprehension at the moment. This is a place that in context is totally 'unphysical,' a true celestial Heaven if you like, a pathway looked to by great spiritual beings such as Abraham, Moses, and Jesus. In truth, Philip, those even in the third and fourth levels often only ever aspire to such heights of progression, as even for them this is truly a distant, angelic place.

"The sixth level is a place of cosmic consciousness where great souls merge in the total oneness of a universal existence. It is perhaps best described in a word that belongs to your Earth plane: God. In truth, Philip, those who exist and progress on the lower levels beneath this have no more understanding of it than you or I, though I have tried to describe it as it has been described to me.

"The seventh level is beyond all comprehension, either materially or physically. I cannot draw unqualified explanations of it, and I tell you in truth, my friend, I do not have the knowledge to explain it. But my learning and teaching has taught me it is what every soul ultimately progresses towards. Ultimately, all experiences in your Earth world and in the spirit levels progress towards a final oneness that is complete and total perfection."

CHAPTER 9

INTERVIEW WITH RICHARD LEWIS

In this communication with Richard Lewis on March 30, 1998, at 9:45 A.M., I tried to ask Richard about many things that would be of interest to us in our world that generally happened in the spirit world:

"Are there animals or pets?"

"Yes, of course. The person that comes over from your world has around him as an individual all things that would please him, including pets and animals. What I am saying to you is this: Evolution never stops taking place in the body or the spirit, and this is applicable both on the Earth plane and in the spirit world. Also, some animals in the higher order are part of a combined group situation. Pets that have been loved and are especially close to human beings certainly progress spiritually and are known here to us, and perhaps in truth you have played a great part in their development with your care and affection for them alongside their companionship with you in a physical way."

"So what you are saying, Richard, is that if I wish to see a pet that had been endeared to me and lost some years ago, in the spirit world it would be there for me?"

"Yes, this is possible," he replied.

"My next question is, do we eat in the spirit world?"

Richard laughed. "It's what's important to you, isn't it

really? You only eat food in the physical world to provide energy for your body, and as you have a spiritual rather than a physical body when you pass over you do not need to sustain it in the same way. For all that, if you had a love of food in the physical being and perhaps enjoyed the experience of eating out, then, yes, it is certainly here for you; whatever you wished or desired would be here, from a banquet to a barbecue. Therefore, you should understand the need for some of us over here to have and eat food, but for many it is not of such importance and belongs to a material nature as yours is. There are succulent fruits and wonderful vegetables that are delicious beyond your imagination, and this is especially so on the level of existence that most of your loved ones will have come to. Basically, as in all things, food and eating would simply be thought of and it would be there for you."

"Tell me, Richard, is it possible for people to have sex after death?"

"Yes, it is possible to have sexual relationships in the spirit world but the need and interrelationship can be very different to that in your world. Here it is often very much a great meeting of minds, and sex is very much more moral and meaningful. Of course, on the very lowest plane there are those driven by sexual perversions and a wish to rape and abuse others, and sometimes those who are evil in this way in your world do retain these vile desires as they pass over to the first level of higher existence. They may try to return to your world to continue their horrible, materialistic ways, perhaps viewing the opposite sex as they bathe or dress or undress themselves, or perhaps achieving excitement by watching the bedroom interactions of couples as they make love. Those who are like them in the body would be especially attracted to them because between the Earth plane and this first level of existence, like attracts like.

"One of the first developments of understanding sexuality, Philip, is this: In the spirit realms, you quickly progress and many are neither male nor female as you would understand sexuality, but combine and blend both genders. This is an important thing for you to understand and pass on to your readers. There are those in the higher realms who have incarnated into male and female beings in your world who emphasize that this is a most important part of progression, that of combined gender orientation."

"How do you spend your daily life, Richard? What do you do? How do you enjoy and occupy your time?"

"The first thing you must remember, Philip, is that time is very different on this side. Of course, when we come over from the Earth plane our interests remain the same. We retain our intellect and interests and of course the prejudices we have learned in that life. The lifestyle you would wish for in this world creates thoughts that would bring about familiarity and pleasure for you. A good example might be that when you are in the spirit world it is a bit like the time in your world when you finish work, retire, and have the opportunity to either reflect on the things you have done in the past, or give time to more interesting hobbies and things you always wished you had the time to do. In this world you are also growing spiritually and there are many other things that are not known to you which would be of interest to you."

"Well then, Richard, I am a great lover of music, everything from popular and rock to classical, so are there opportunities to go to such events in the spirit world?"

Richard laughed at this enquiry. "Yes, of course. Only recently myself and several friends attended a wonderful concert where many of the great composers performed. But perhaps of even more interest to you is that they have many more new works to perform; indeed, many of them influence those who are true mediums in your world to be aware of them. You may also feel that the light and laser shows that are new in your world belong only to you, but here we have similar experiences of lights and vibrations that perfectly blend with the music being performed to create entertainment that is most ecstatic to the listener."

"So you are saying that the great musicians carry on their work in the spirit world?"

"Yes, of course," said Richard. "And those you would call geniuses in your understanding also. The scientists or those with brilliant inventive minds do not finish their work at death, as some of those in your existence would believe, but carry on their work in the spirit realms. I tell you in truth, Philip, many of them try to and do inspire those who are like-minded in your world and continue to make new inventions and scientific progress. Of course we still have great houses of learning or universities, as you may better understand them, where the great thinkers and those of wonderful intellects (whom some of you in your world thought of as dead) gather and continue inventing far in advance of your scientists on the Earth plane, yet always, unconsciously at least, trying to inspire those below to the benefit of those in your world. I tell you in truth, Philip, many of the discoveries that your wise ones make come from the inspiration of our wise ones in the spirit world.

"Look for the many examples of the great discoveries that have been made throughout your history and notice that although one great mind has discovered it, many others at that time are chasing that discovery also and are very close to it. Does that not give you a hint of the inspiration from those of us above?"

"One thing I find difficult, Richard, and I would ask you that if this is so, why do those above not always influence us to be good so there would be no wickedness in this world?"

Again, Richard chuckled. "A wiser one than I told you many years ago that you always have free will, that it is part of your progression."

"Do people sleep in the spirit world, Richard, and if so, for how long?"

"As you have been told many times, everything is just a thought away, including sleep, which of course was a pleasurable experience in the Earthly body, both relaxing and enjoyable. Yes, many of us choose to sleep on this side of existence, but probably for shorter periods for there is so much to do and experience the minute your thoughts take you in another direction. For some, often the sleeping time is when their thoughts are sent towards your world, and it is very much when unconscious communication occurs between the two worlds, between loved ones from both sides if you like, by communicating in a confined dream state."

"Can you travel in the spirit world in the way we travel in our world? Do you have cars, motorcycles, trains?"

"Well, yes, of course, Philip. As I have explained to you, anything that is part of your understanding as you come over and you think of it would be there for you, and if you enjoyed traveling and moving around in this way then of course you can do so. Much of my traveling both in England and the New Land was of course on horseback. "

"Do you mean America?"

"Yes, indeed, America. Whereas my good friend, John, often travels around in an old car that he calls a 'shooting brake.' It's a strange sort of vehicle really—half car and half wooden. You would find it very funny to look at. But as I have told you we travel around in this way because it has been a pleasure to us in other existences. Equally, when we wish to be somewhere quickly, we just think of that place and are there. Thoughts are powerful things my friend!"

"Well then, Richard, do you have villages and cities and countries the way we have in our world?"

"Yes, exactly the same. There are billions of people here who carry on existences in the various levels of understanding in much the same way it would be on your own Earth plane. But as you would build with bricks and mortar, we build all our great structures with thoughts, but visually the perception of them is the same."

"I would like to ask you a question that is very interesting to me. How do you communicate with us from your world?"

Richard laughed. "That's a funny question from a medium, Philip. How do you communicate with us?"

"Is that a serious question, Richard?"

"Of course it is!" he replied.

"Well, I just bring myself into a relaxed state, usually say a little prayer to myself, and open myself up and have a wish to see and communicate with those who would like to communicate with me."

"And, Philip, that is exactly what we do on this side, but

of course there are some of us who, like you and your friends, meet and sit together in seances and circles of development. We are aware there are mediums in your world who are good and genuine and others who are known to us as charlatans and frauds. We would think of them and our words would be with them, perhaps unconsciously to start with, but when you sit quietly and relax, as you put it, the communication placed there for you will come through. It really is as simple as that—a combining of thoughts."

"Richard, from the things you have said to me it would appear that you have lived several lives, including time spent on my Earth plane. Is that so?"

"Yes, I have chosen several times to come back and live lives in your experience to gain wisdom and knowledge that would help me do the work I am now doing, which is trying hard to inspire people like yourself on the Earth plane."

"Who makes the choice about whether you can come back or not?"

"The choice is always your own, and making it is all part of your progression. For example, there are those who wish to help the disabled and the sick or those who wish to have political power to be good and help others, but unless you came back and lived the physical experiences of the suffering of the disabled, or the pressures of the politician, how could you understand and influence from above? In one of my lives, many, many centuries ago in time as you understand it, I was a wise man. In another life, a medicine man. These are people very much like yourself, Philip, and that is why I am drawn to come into conversation with you now. But I have also lived the life of a materialist."

"Therefore, the person who makes the decision about whether you come back is entirely yourself?"

"Yes, entirely," confirmed Richard.

"Can you tell me about the people who are in charge in your world?"

"That is a difficult question to answer for first you have to understand there are seven different levels of existence. Do you understand this?"

"Well, I have had communications that would seem to prove that to be the case," I answered.

"Let us talk of the second level of existence then, Philip. This is where many of your loved ones would come to and, of course, in their earthly bodies they would become used to being advised, guided, managed, if you like, by people in authority, by governments, leaders, or teachers. If they are comfortable with this then their thoughts will provide that for them. Others who are slightly more progressed will be aware of this and take on the roles supportive to the thought patterns of these people, or if you like simple terms, become the bosses."

"What about the higher levels of existence then?" I asked.

"In the higher realms there are great wise ones who have come together in groups to work and advise and help others. They are not our 'bosses,' in your general sense of understanding, but are people who would guide in such a way with great wisdom and knowledge that it would be accepted. But even they are guided by those above them in other higher levels of existence, which is the abode of those you would describe as prophets, saints, and great beings. Even they are ultimately moving towards being part of that complete oneness which is in the seventh level of understanding. They also are governed from above, so to speak. Therefore, everyone and everything is answerable to the one great upper source or force.

"This is extremely difficult for you to understand and comprehend, and in this type of communication it is difficult to put it over to you, but as you think on the words I have said to you great understanding will be there for you. It is known to us on this side of existence that millions of people will read this book that you and Hans Holzer are putting together. We are glad for the understanding that will be given to the readers."

CHAPTER 10

CONVERSATION WITH PETER JACKSON

This communication came from Peter Jackson, who in his last life had lived as an officer in the U.S. Cavalry at the time of the Great Indian Wars and had spent much of his time living in Montana or a place possibly called Montana Bay. Peter contacted and made communication with me on April 1, 1998, at 7:15 P.M., wishing to tell others in our world what it was like in his world, the spirit world.

Peter started off by telling me that we on Earth actually live in a world that is a "positive/negative place" and not the first level of existence as some psychics would have us believe. He said we are given the choice to be good or bad, whereas, in the spirit world, we are always guided and helped to continually progress, never to step backwards. Everyone has someone who cares for and loves them in the spirit world and whom they can be close to and be comforted by. You would never have a feeling of being alone or unloved in the spirit world.

Peter said, "Philip, you will have many people come to you wanting advice or explanations or words of comfort about their friends, partners, and loved ones who have come up to this level of existence. People in your world will always worry if they are okay, if they are happy, and in truth, I must tell you they always are. Never have I known anyone who, when the astral cord separated their spirit from their body, has tried to reconnect it, for the perfect light of our world is far too attractive. In the spirit world there is little room for hate, greed, jealousy or unkindness; yet in other ways it is quite similar to life on Earth."

At this stage I asked Peter, "How do we know when we are coming to the spirit world, and what happens when we get to the Other Side? Is there a hierarchy of power? Will the mayor or sheriff be waiting to hand us a key to Heaven?"

This made Peter laugh, and I suppose I was being comical in my questioning. "When you get to the Other Side and are accepted into the spirit world, there will be a time required for you to adjust to your new surroundings; but you must remember, Philip, you exist as a completely different person. Your perception and reality develop quickly to a new dimension that you are living and operating within, but in truth, progression and enlightenment start to take place. Of course, your spiritual world will be very much the same as you would have known it in your Earth life; all the things that gave you pleasure, even physical, are no more than a thought pattern away for you."

Again, Peter laughed. "In the body I often smoked and chewed tobacco, and in the early days of my progression, my pipe and chewing tobacco were always there for me. In the physical world I also played a mean fiddle and enjoyed a glass of bourbon, and in my early progression, they would also be there for me. But things we have here soon become more attractive to us, and I wanted to quickly move on to higher levels of understanding. Maybe at some time later I could come back for a further experience of your world."

"Peter, can I ask you a question here: Is it true that many people have had past lives?"

"If that question was truly from you, Philip, it would make me angry, because you know the answer to that yourself; but as it is a question for your book then I will tell you plainly, everyone who is on the physical plane now has lived before."

"So everyone continually comes back?"

"Yes, to some extent that is true, but those who exist on

the higher planes are much progressed from the time they were on your plane and will probably never come onto the Earth plane again. They have a very high level of consciousness and elevated form of pure spirit. Their understanding of things is way beyond my comprehension and development, let alone those of you on the Earth plane. On occasions, their essence may draw close to your world, but they would come in a different form to the one you would recognize in association with your own energies. More often than not, they come for their own progression as much as for yours. If a descriptive word would be required, Philip, perhaps the one I would choose from your world would be 'angel'; but they are not the angels from your religious books. They are the entities nearest to the God light and come to give an overall beneficial influencing pattern to the whole of planet Earth. Many who call themselves mediums and psychics speak of commanding the guardian angels, and other such statements. In truth, this is not possible from your world. It is not the place to command such beings and they are far beyond and above the command of earthly mortals."

"Peter, this is very interesting, but what I really want to know for the readers of this book is what is it like in the spirit world, generally speaking?"

"But I have already told you, Philip, it is very similar to the Earth world. We have our buildings and houses, restaurants, theaters, buildings of every sort you would recognize from your time on Earth. Everything is the same, Philip, but built in your mind, and it is a perfect place. Of course we are still very aware of our loved ones in your world and will direct help and guidance towards them to make your difficult earthly lives perhaps a little easier to bear. We continue on in the same way we did in the physical world, still very much influenced in the early days by our former existence. Basically, we carry on much the same as we did below, and there are many times when we are close to your world. That is why we can sometimes manifest or pass messages on through your mediums to guide and help you in the same way that I speak to you now."

Peter laughed at this stage and went on. "Or perhaps, if I am honest, the reason we come back so often is because this world is so similar to your world that we get a little homesick! I jest, Philip, as you can see we still retain our sense of humor in the spirit world!"

At this stage I again indicated to Peter how important it was for the readers to know exactly what it was like in the spirit world. He started to get a little angry with me. "How many times do I have to tell you Philip? It is just the same as what you have below."

"All right then Peter, let me ask you something else. Tell me about the individual's spirit guides."

"Well," he answered, "I'll tell you this much, Philip. Completely contrary to the popular belief of so-called mediums and psychics, a guide is only there really to help in difficult and, if you like, progressive stages of your life. No one, not even the most famed of mediums or psychics, continually has a spirit guide with them. If they tell you they do, they are false mediums and you should not believe them.

"Generally, the guides, who come from higher realms, have had experiences similar to the experiences you have in your own physical life and in order for them to progress without having to come back and face the earthly life that you do, a spirit guide will steer others through difficulties to bring about Karma and progression for themselves as well as you. Once that pathway has been faced and you have 'learned the lesson,' any number of other guides may choose to help as and when appropriate. Of course, the psychic ones in your world continually talk of tuning into the guidance of others. Do you know there have also been guides in your world, great prophets if you like, who, interestingly, give a similar or the same message: love one another and look for fairness between men and women. Was that not the words of the great Jesus?

"In your own time did not people such as Mahatma Gandhi, John Lennon, Mother Theresa, and Princess Diana preach such peace and love between mankind? Of course they did. But the guides give their guidance and help from a very high level of existence and are not always on tap the way some mediums would have you believe they are. Many of them are moving close in their progression to what you would call God, and in your world they certainly have the ability to change things round and make things better for you even in the most difficult situations."

"Okay, Peter, but I ask you again, what is it like in the spirit world?"

Peter laughed again. "Philip, no one in your life would be able to understand the conditions that are in the spirit dimension. You can only be conscious of physical experiences that are relevant to your physical life, and no one in the human, physical body can have the complete mental ability to see colors that are beyond the colors that are known in your existence, within your spectrum. Let me put it like this to you: I can promise you that in the spirit world there are beautiful flowers and wonderful colors, but if I was to say to you that in this world not only would you see these beautiful flowers but you could talk to them—could you accept that?"

"Can you talk to the flowers?" I asked.

"Actually, I have not tried," he replied laughing. "So it is difficult for me to answer that question. But I will tell you this, if that would give great pleasure to someone who came up to us, then it would be a reality to them!"

"This is difficult for me, Peter. I live in a world where there are massive skyscrapers, juggernaut lorries, and more cars than the roads can handle. Are you saying to me that when I come to your existence these things will still be there?"

"Yes, I am. If these things give you pleasure, then they would be there. However, if you felt you would be much happier somewhere more balanced and relaxed that had none of these things, then that would be your abode in the spirit world."

CHAPTER 11

INTERVIEW WITH JANET

Janet contacted me on April 3, 1998, at 8:45 P.M. and made communication many times over the years following, but in this particular conversation she came through hoping to explain, perhaps even answer, a few questions at my prompting, about what life would be like for an ordinary person on the Other Side of existence in the spirit world. This is what she had to say and these are her responses to some of my questions:

"Janet," I asked, "what is your everyday existence like? What is the spirit world like?"

"Well, Philip, the spirit world, as you call it, is different things to different people with different cultures, but basically it's a good place; and whatever I wanted in my material life is also here for me—my heart's desires, if you like."

"But what about when you are away from a loved one or have left behind someone like a husband, wife, boyfriend, or girlfriend?"

"Well, you see, Philip, in the spirit world we would always be preparing a place for that reunion, so the loss would be felt between us, but still we would be working towards certain reunion."

"Do you have a job, Janet?"

"Yes, I'm a teacher. I have been a teacher in the body and this is something I enjoyed, and continue to do so here."

"What is your school like?" I asked.

"Much the same as when I was alive. Most of my students are very young children. They need to be taught to operate within the existence they live in the same as any little child would be wherever they were."

"So it's not a matter of teaching them to read and write, you know, 'the three R's'?"

"Well, yes, strangely enough, we do teach those things, but also a greater wisdom of spirituality and love for each other. Often we teach them about the people who belong to them in the physical body. Some of these children will have been aborted, or perhaps passed over at the time of birth, or they are very young, and they are extremely interested in their parents and the things that happen in your world."

"Do you have a partner in the spirit world, Janet?"

"No, as yet the one I have chosen to spend much of my existence with is still in your world, although I do have many friends of both sexes."

"From the way you speak, Janet, I would assume you are a fairly young woman."

"Yes, that is right. As you would understand ages, I am about thirty-five," she replied.

"Do you ever feel a physical relationship would be nice for you?" I asked.

"No, in truth that is not something that appeals to me. But I know the question you are looking to ask me. Would that be possible in our world if I wished it to be so? And the answer to that is, yes, it would, but it is not something I would wish for at this stage of my progression."

"Can I ask you how you communicate with us in our world?"

"Yes, of course. This is done through what you would term the guides on this side."

"What are guides?"

"These are people who are wise and have progressed from the lower levels of our world and are both psychically and spiritually knowledgeable of both worlds—of course, much more of our side—and they are individuals who facilitate communication between our world and yours. Basically, they are people like yourself in your world: mediums. These guides pass our word through to you in much the same way that a radio receiver works in your world; sometimes they speak themselves through trance mediums."

"Are you a guide, Janet?"

"Yes, I am, and that is why I can speak to you directly and help you with this book."

"Then why has no one else written a book like this?"

"The perfect communication that you make with the spirit world, Philip, is a special gift that you have and is not available to many though other guides have made this knowledge known to mediums and have passed on great philosophy. But it is a difficult thing to do. Remember, your world is a material world and time dependent, and for us in the spirit world this can sometimes cause difficulties, especially when you have not been in a physical body for some time, perhaps hundreds of years!"

"Janet, even though I am a medium, death scares me at times, and I am sure it is the same for other people in our world."

"It shouldn't," she replied. "Not someone like you, Philip. I do understand your position, yet death and passing up to our level are basically very similar to physical birth and coming into your existence. In the first instance, the spirit simply leaves the body, and in the second, it enters a physical body and it is the most natural of transitions."

"Then may I ask you another question that comes to mind? Do you have doctors and nurses and hospitals in the spirit world?"

"Of course we do. We have wonderful doctors and nurses and magnificent hospitals and medical centers and this is where many in their transition are taken to as they pass over if the transition to our world has been difficult. Many of our doctors would treat you with a method that you would find quite similar to hypnosis whereby you are placed in a relaxing sleep until the whole of your body is perfect again. This is often why people feel disappointed when they do not get communication from a loved one for what, in your lifetime, may seem a very long time. You should remember that it may be that loved one is in this sleep-type state. I would remind you again that time is different on our side from yours. Of course, if you have spiritual and psychic knowledge and understand our world, the way someone like yourself would, Philip, you would have no such difficulties at all in coming over. Basically, as I have told you before, you would step into our world in very much the way you perceive your own world, except you would see it has much more to offer for your development."

"Janet, could you describe a hospital to me?"

"Well, yes. It is very much like the hospitals you know on Earth except many of them are built of beautiful glass-like bricks and all of the treatments are mind-oriented. There is no suffering, no pain, and all of our patients work towards an ultimate 'cure' as you would call it, though 'oneness' is a more appropriate word."

"What about those who come over very late in years? If you are ninety or one hundred years of age, are you like that in the spirit world, if we perceive the spirit world to be like our own?"

"Yes, it would be when you first came over, Philip, but I will tell you this. Very quickly these people in older years start moving back towards the years of their prime."

"Are you saying you get younger in the spirit world then?"

"Yes, this is often the case; not always, but generally the case. If you would like to think of it in terms of your physical life, you would probably feel at your optimal performance, somewhere between the ages of about twenty and thirty-five. Generally this is what people work towards. I would also tell you this: Babies very quickly grow to that same optimum age that I have spoken of. Therefore, when a mother thinks that a little child she has lost is still a little child, this is not always the case. Sometimes in the space of two, three, or perhaps five years (this is as best as I can describe it in your time), that child may have grown to a young man or woman in their years of optimal ability; though when the parent first comes to our world, let me emphasize, the parent's perception of that little lost child will be as it was when the parent first gave it back to us."

"It is often said, Janet, that when we pass to your level a loved one will appear to take us over. Therefore, if ages change and people work towards this optimal age of say, thirty, how would you recognize your mother or your father if they came to take you over at your death?"

This made Janet laugh. "Yes, I do know what you are saying. As others will have told you and as I will tell you again, when you first make your progression to what we call a different level of existence, that which is your heart's desire would be there for you. Therefore, if it were your mother or father, you would see them as you remember them shortly before they passed over. It is like a jigsaw, Philip: everything fits into place when the overall picture is set before you."

"Janet, where is the spirit world?"

"It's all around you, Philip. We are in a dimension that is permanently in and around your physical world, yet we exist on a different vibration or frequency, if you like, that does not change in the spatial sense."

"So what you are saying is that in a way you are around us all the time, or those that we call dead are around us all the time?"

"Yes, and unless you are a medium, such as yourself, with clairvoyant abilities, you will not see or hear us; although, of course, in your world millions do, yet will not believe what they see or hear with their own eyes or ears. As I and others who will communicate with you and will tell you, the early levels of the spirit world and your world are very similar. Indeed, this is why when many come over from your side they find it totally unacceptable that they are dead—their environment is so similar and painted by the life they lived in their physical existence. This afterlife, as you call it, in its early stages is absolutely *your* perception and relevant to what *you* did and enjoyed in your physical life, and although it is part of the progression of your people to learn things for themselves, I will tell you that if they are kind, good, and generous people, then their awakening will be in a beautiful place that is relevant to them. Whereas if their life is very physically and materialistically oriented, then this is the kind of place that will await them when they first come over."

"Janet, do the people we know physically as being famous for their good or bad deeds carry on doing these things in your realms? Are the film stars still film stars for example, or the inventors still inventors?"

"Yes, of course they are, and they do sometimes carry on with things they enjoy, and they still influence those in your world. Do you think that a brain such as Einstein's would be allowed to die away just because his physical body had stopped functioning? Think about it, Philip. Of course they carry on, and equally as important, people I know have contacted you, or will contact you, such as Marilyn Monroe and Elvis Presley, who still wish to bring pleasure and entertain people as they do in our world, and to send back influences to your world."

"What about disabilities, Janet—people who only had one arm or leg? This would be the body they were used to so would they still be like this when they first came to the spirit world?"

"The answer is yes, but progression quickly takes place and soon they would be whole again and in perfect health in both body and mind; and, as I have already told you, they would quickly move towards an optimal time in their body."

"What if they were born without arms or legs, what then?"

"No matter; they would quickly become whole and perfect in every way, except perhaps when presenting themselves in their recognizable form to those who would come over in later years."

"Janet, you've told me you are a teacher, and you've told me about your school and friendships. You've described the hospitals. Just simply describe the spirit world for the readers."

"That is impossible, for as you know there are many levels, and the spirit world, in its complete context, is unbelievably vast and unexplainable, and in truth it is not fully understandable to me for I am only on the third level of existence."

"So you are saying there are parts of the spirit world that you don't know about?"

"Yes, Philip, that is right. Did not the great Lord Jesus tell us in his incarnation on the physical Earth, 'In my Father's house there are many mansions'?"

"So this means then there are seven or eight levels of existence such as other communicants have told me about?"

"It means what it says: There are many mansions and you can only have limited knowledge without moving up to these different levels."

"So you can't tell me what the spirit world is like in its entirety?"

"No, I can only tell you about the spirit world I live in and I have done so; but I cannot tell you about the levels above me any more than you can tell me about this level that I exist in!"

"Okay, Janet, let me go back to some other questions, then. Do you eat food, and what type of food do you eat?"

"You are back to the physical thing of when we first come over, Philip. What you wish to be there is there. But as you progress higher in the spirit world all you need to do is absorb energy, as everyone and everything is sustained in perfection."

"What about sex then?"

"In truth, Philip, sex is only important when you are on the first levels of existence and you are still close to the Earth plane. This is why many partners return to the Earth plane and wish to be close to their former partners. Physical sex does not really happen in our world once we have progressed, but it is more a union, a combination of minds coming together."

"Okay, then, who is in charge over there, who is ultimately the boss?"

"Again that is hard to explain to you, but if you mean like presidents, prime ministers, and those who would take charge of others, then they would carry on in much the same roles in our world, in the lower levels, as they did when they were in body, for this is the special gift they have. But ultimately, the 'boss,' the title you use, would be God. We, in these lower levels of progression, see God in much the same way that you would see God on your Earth plane, and we are still on the same spiritual quest to understand this greatness in just the same way that you are. Basically we believe in God the same as you, but that God that you speak of would be the very highest of those mansions that Jesus of Nazareth spoke of. For most of us, this is as long a way into the future of our progression as it is for you."

"So how do you spend your time then? Do you have hobbies and the like?"

"Well, yes, of course. When you first come over to this level of existence your interests remain the same, a bit like retirement, if you like. You don't have a job to go to every day, and you have time to do the things you want to, but, by and large, you are still drawn back to the things that were interesting to you when you were in a working life. If you were interested in golf, we have unbelievable golf courses. If you wish to play tennis, we have wonderful tennis courts. If you like to write, or are interested in poetry, that is there for you as well.

"Last week I attended a wonderful classical music concert where several of the great composers gave a performance, and I tell you, Philip, these composers are still here and still work; everyone from Beethoven, to the Beatle, John Lennon. They are still here carrying on, performing in the way they would in the physical. Such talent does not end with death. We also have great cities here where great minds gather together to work and discuss inventions and things that would progress the cosmos. Indeed, often through your mediums passing this wisdom on back to your Earth plane, many of the great discoveries in history in your world have come from the spirit world when a great mind over here has influenced or overshadowed a great mind still operating in your world."

"What about bad discoveries then, such as the atomic or hydrogen bomb? Was that influenced from above?"

"No, Philip, generally such discoveries are entirely from your world, though often regretted by the inventor as he or she progresses."

"Janet, tell me more of the cities and towns that you say these people operate or exist within."

"Do you have a map of America, Philip, or perhaps of your own country, England?"

"Yes, I do."

"Then these are much the same. We create cities, villages, roads, towns, places such as these, but they are very much like the places you exist in."

"So you travel by cars, trains, planes, and similar things then?"

"Philip, I have told you many times that in these first levels of existence in our progression everything is exactly the same as it is in your world. Of course, we have the ability to travel by thought but we have very little sense of time over here. Time is not the same in our world as it is in yours, and we carry on much the same way until we make progression to higher levels of understanding. Then the cities, planes, and trains and the things we have known in your physical world and in our lower spiritual world are of no further use to us."

"Then tell me about these worlds."

"I cannot, for I know as little about them as you do, for though your world and my world are very close together only on a different vibrational level, you will know how difficult it is to communicate for most people.

"I tell you in truth, Philip, it is equally as difficult on the levels two and three to communicate with the higher levels. However, if it is their wish for you to have knowledge for this book, it is my understanding a way could be found. But I must leave you now, Philip, for this afternoon I am visiting one of the great cities I have told you about and I hope to play a little tennis later on this evening."

"Are you joking with me there, Janet, or are you serious?"

"Of course I'm not joking with you, Philip. I loved to shop when I was in your world and I loved to play tennis and very little has changed for me in those ways at the moment."

"Thank you, Janet."

"Thank you, Philip. Goodbye."

CHAPTER 12

CONVERSATION WITH GEORGE SMITH

George Smith came through and spoke these words to me on April 20, 1998, at 2:45 P.M.:

"Good day, Philip, I am very interested in the book that Hans Holzer and you are writing. I am sure that it will be very popular; indeed, many people over here, like myself, have expressed an interest in contributing to it and seeing the finished project."

"Are you serious, George? Are there really other people on the Other Side equally as interested in this book as we are?"

"Yes, of course," he answered. "It is an opportunity for people in your world to know what the spirit world is like."

"Tell me about your life in spirit, George."

"Well, it is very much like it was when I was in the body, as all the other communicators will have told you I am sure."

"That is true," I answered him. "By the way, what did you do in the body?"

"That's not really very important, but I will tell you I was an American and spent a lot of my life as a soldier, a horse soldier."

"Where did you die then?"

"Again, that is not very important, but I died in one of the most important Indian battles of all—the one they called the

Battle of the Little Big Horn, or Custer's Last Stand, I think you call it in your world. But I have no wish to tell you about that really; it has no importance, except that I learned that war has no meaning and afterward people tell lies about battles. When you meet your enemy on this side, you find you have much in common even if you have been taught they were savages."

"When did you die, George?"

"June 26, 1876, not even forty years of age, and I am thinking about coming back for another life, you know."

"What do you do now?"

"Well, when I first came to this world I could barely read and write, like lots of soldiers. We weren't the smart, clever people you would think we were. Often we were almost illiterate and very undisciplined. While I have been here I have gone to the schools we have here, wonderful places where you just think about knowledge and it comes through and is implanted in your mind. I have also gone to our universities and studied philosophy and music."

"Did you play music when you were in the body?"

"No, not really, but I always liked to listen to people play their fiddles and instruments like that, and found once I arrived here I could learn to do those things too, and have done so!"

"So you are saying to me then that you can achieve anything in the spirit world?"

"Yes, of course, within reason, you can do anything that you want."

"You say 'within reason;' what do you mean by that?"

"Well, some of us would have wished to progress to higher levels but have learned that we must experience other things on this level we exist in and maybe come back to your world and live more lives before we can move to that place."

"Are all people equal in your world? You mention the Battle of the Little Big Horn, and that you lost your life there, so what is Colonel Custer like there? I know it is a strange thing I am asking you but it helps us to know about these things."

"Custer is Custer. Much the same as he was in life—bit of a braggart, bit of a show-off—yet often he keeps the company of Crazy Horse. He was one of the Indian chiefs who led his people into battle that day, though Crazy Horse is much wiser these days and seems very interested in helping all of the Indian people in your world. You are being coy with me, Philip, for I know he has communicated with you!"

"Er, I would like to believe so! I would like to believe so."

"You know so. In fact, he is standing here right now."

"Is he really? Can I speak to you, Crazy Horse?"

"Yes of course you can," answered Crazy Horse. "But don't ask me about Little Big Horn, for that is history and in the past, and many lessons were to be learned there by the red man and the white man. I am sick of people saying this was an opportunity for the Indians to have banded together against the white soldiers, the pony soldiers. This could never have happened. Do not forget the Crows and the Arikaras. They fought on the side of the pony soldiers and too much bad blood existed between us and the Crow people to ever join together against the whites. The only thing that came out of the Big Horn was dignity for my people, for a short period."

"Okay, then, Crazy Horse, can you tell me about your life in spirit."

"No, my son, that is not what I wish to do. I would just wish to say hello to you today and wish you and your friend, Holzer, well in this project that you are trying to bring together to try to help all people, and with those words I will wish you farewell."

"Hmm, that was a bit short and sweet, George!"

"It was, but you were greatly honored by his presence."

"Yes, I appreciate that. I don't want to be rude here, but a lot of the communications that I am getting through is almost like a conversation that is very interesting but seems to be just between myself and the person I speak to; but what we really need is for you to tell us about the Other Side and exactly what happens there."

"That is very difficult, Philip. My life is much the same as it was in the physical, except that I can be anywhere in the twinkling of a thought and do anything that I want to achieve. That is the main difference between your world and ours. Over here, anything is possible with just the slightest thought."

"How did you contact me today to give me this interview for which I am grateful?"

"We are aware of the things you do in your world. There are those who would spread the word in a media-type way, much the way it is spread in your world. This book you are writing is known of on our side and I would wish to contribute to it."

"I am very grateful to you, but tell me how you got through to me today. Did you have to use a medium between the two worlds the way I am often a medium for other people from our world to yours?"

"There are people who work in that way; but of course we are more developed and as I have told you, just to think of something would put it in place. Therefore, if I think of you, then you would be on my thought vibration. Actually this is the way we communicate with each other in this world as well. We just think of you and then our communication somehow goes through to you; but more often than not, because you are not advanced in this form (you might want to call it a form of telepathy if you like), you have to have a medium like yourself between the two worlds for it to be understood and received. From our end, we just think of you and that thought structure comes through to your world."

"You have spoken a lot of war. Are there battles in the spirit world?"

"No, there are no wars in this world. The only way we take part in wars is to try to influence and stop the people in your world from having the wars that continually go on which achieve nothing."

"So the spirit world never influences man to do evil then?"

"Not from this level—the second level and above—though there are people below us in the spirit world, below my level in a first level of existence, who find pleasure in seeing men and women hurting and fighting each other; but they are the people who would create evil in the physical world as well. So if you know such people as these who come over in the early days in their passing, they would certainly influence people towards war in your world. But there is no war in the spirit world above that level of existence."

"George, this might sound like a silly question, but, are you a married person and could you have children in the spirit world?"

"No, this is not the way it is with us over here," George laughed. "Relationships are different in the spirit world. This is true; I am with my wife who came to me many years after the date I lost my life in the physical sense; but I also have a closeness with another lady that I spent many years with in the spirit world. There is no physical marriage or union in the way you are asking me and we do not have children in this world. The babies, or 'sparks of life,' as we would call them, are immediately conceived from spirit unification and are what incarnates in your world."

"Oh, I see. That is an interesting point that I would like to be clarified for me: the results of unions in your world result in the babies coming into our world?"

"Yes, in a manner of speaking, though we do not have sex in the way that you would in your physical existence to create that life. It is more a perfect communion of minds that creates an incarnation."

"But could you have sex if you wanted to?"

"Er, yes, we could, and again, as I have already said, in the levels of the spirit world under us they do, and often draw close to your world as well for that very reason; but we have reached a stage of combining with the opposite gender in a much more spiritual way, though great pleasure is found in doing that."

"Do you grow older in your world, George?"

"No, not really. Quite often we grow younger; in fact, to an age when we were in our optimal state of health."

"Do you have hospitals and places like that? Do you ultimately die the way we do before you go up a level?"

"We do have hospitals, but they are mostly for the people who first come over to us and come straight to the second level and need to recuperate and get better, to get ready and prepared to exist in this new dimension. We do not have death, as you speak of and know in your world, before we decide to go to the next higher level or come back to Earth for a rebirth; but it is more an understanding and a knowledge of what is completely right for the individual spirit being. It is not a physical, painful death in the way you experience on Earth, though I would remind you, as you have asked the question, that death as you speak of it does not really exist anyway."

"Are there entertainments in your world? Do you ride horses or drive cars as we do in our world?"

This made George laugh again. "As others have told you, anywhere you wish to be you just think of it and you can be there; so in truth you wouldn't need a car or a horse in our world. But if you enjoyed these things you would simply think of them and they would be there for you. This is how we exist: a thought-structured pattern that makes anything available to you, though I often enjoy riding and do that very thing. I also enjoy films, which became popular long after I left my physical body, but I enjoy watching some of the great film stars perform."

"Can I ask who you enjoy watching and who you have seen perform in the spirit world?"

"Yes, certainly. Names that you will know such as James Dean, Marilyn Monroe, Errol Flynn, Mae West. Not only do I see them perform, but I am honored to speak and communicate with them. There is no real social structure over here that stops you from being anything, anywhere, or from communicating with anyone you wish to. Everything is known to us over here. I know, for instance, that you know descendants of the legendary Western sheriff Wyatt Earp's family; but did you know he has written a book over here, one that is being made into a film and musical? Did you know that?"

"George, are you joking with me or are you serious?"

"Absolutely serious, Philip! Do you not know the descendants of Wyatt Earp in the physical?"

"Well, actually, yes it's true, I do; so I suppose it does make sense what you are saying."

"There you go then. Life goes on over here much the same as it does in your world. For instance, Stan Laurel and Oliver Hardy have just made a wonderful film that is very successful in our world. Harry Houdini, the great magician, whom I know you have spoken to as well, also continues his work over here entertaining people. Has he not told you so?"

"Er, no. When I communicated with Mr. Houdini it was on other matters."

"And I know what that matter is, but I tell you he still performs here, as does Sir Oliver Lodge, who brought a great deal of interest in spiritualism into Houdini's life in the physical. Sir Oliver Lodge does much work here and prefers to be called just Oliver Lodge!"

"You have spoken of some very famous people there, George. I am sure the people of my world will be glad to know they have not stopped doing their wonderful work just because they have passed through the veil of death."

"I don't use that word Philip, but I know what you mean. Yes, of course, they carry on."

"Can you tell me about some of the more religious people whom we have known in the physical, like Jesus for instance?"

"No, Philip, I cannot tell of those such as Jesus, for he is on a much higher level than I am; you must understand that. He and his kind are so wonderful and are still so high above us that there is very little difference in our understanding from your understanding of those beings, except we know they are there and are part of something that is great above us."

"Thank you for giving me that information. Is there anything else at all you would like to tell me about the spirit world?"

"It is very difficult, you know."

"I know it is. I am finding it very difficult to sort this out for myself, but this is what Hans has asked me to ask you."

"You see, the difficulty is that the communications you will make will be mostly from the level I operate within, and that world, as we think of our world, is very similar to yours. What Hans and you may be asking me about and what you are interested in, have to do with the worlds above this; but you have to make communication with those people to do that, and this is very difficult. In truth, all the communication, or the large majority that comes through to your world, comes from ordinary, everyday people like myself, who still have a great interest in your world. There are mediums like you, Philip, who have wisdom come through from what people speak of as the higher guides. When it is right you may have no doubt they will influence people like me and you to tell us what we need to know to progress. With those words I wish you, Hans Holzer, and your work with this book to be guided by the light of enlightenment, and may you both be helped by those in the higher realms. Goodbye, Philip."

"Goodbye, George."

CHAPTER 13

THE WORDS OF PRINCESS DIANA

This communication with Princess Diana came on April 29, 1998, at 3:30 P.M.:

"Hello, Diana. How are you? Are you well and happy?"

"Yes, I am happy. I have never been more happy than I am now, Philip, but of course I do miss my boys, Wills and Harry, and as you will understand, I am never very far from them in spirit."

"Of course, I do understand, Ma'am."

"Never call me Ma'am, Philip. Always call me Diana."

"I am sorry, Diana, that is very nice of you. Diana, you know I am writing this book, so is it possible that you could tell me about your life in spirit."

"It is, but I am afraid if you were to ask me certain questions about my passing over then it will be very difficult for me to speak without bringing great shock and unhappiness to the world."

"What do you mean by that, Diana?"

"As I say, it is very difficult for me to speak, Philip, except to say it was not my time and I should not have come over to this side of existence as I did."

"Are you saying you were murdered?"

"All I am saying, Philip, is that I came to the spirit world before it was my time. I always told Sarah that one day something would happen to one of us, where we would go up in a helicopter or something similar and it would just go 'bang!' and that would be the end of one or both of us. Basically, my words proved to be the truth."

"By Sarah, do you mean the Duchess of York?"

"Yes, I do, and I would wish her to know she is still my best friend, always was and always will be, the only one I could ever really talk to and know that what I said would not be used against me or repeated in the future."

"You seem very bitter, Diana. Are you angry and unhappy with people in our physical world?"

"Yes, Philip, of course I am. People I cared for and shared privacies with are now speaking about me in a public way. I am also disappointed with those I truly loved. When I came to them in my bodily life and asked them for help, they turned me away. Now those same people would have you believe they are my greatest allies."

"Are you speaking of family or friends, Diana?"

"Unfortunately, Philip, I have to say to you that I am speaking of both. I never chose wisely in my life where friends were concerned, and deserved many of the things that happened to me. Basically, they let me down. But your family, your closest family, should always be there for you, don't you think?"

"Yes, Diana, I feel that is true."

"But let's not dwell on these things. We have talked about these things in the past, in a more private way, haven't we, and I know you will never tell the things I have told you."

"It is true, Diana, I will not. But may I ask you what your life is like in spirit?"

"As I have said, it is wonderful. I have never been more happy. Many I care about are very close to me, especially my father who was there waiting for me to take me over from your world to this world. I am also very close and friendly with Dodi. He and I are going to do much work to try and help you in the physical world to love and care for one another. I was so surprised by how much people seemed to love me. Seeing all the flowers and tributes left at the various sites throughout the world was really very touching, and I would ask those in your world to show the same love and care to my two boys. That is the most important thing to me. Also, I am so sorry for Dodi's father; he was always good and kind to me, Wills, and Harry. Whatever anyone might have said, I liked him very much and I'm sure he liked me too, and the story he speaks of regarding a ring is the truth."

"May I ask you again, Diana, what your everyday life is like then, what you are doing? Excuse me, Ma'am, but do you still have a film-star sort of life rather than a princess existence?"

"Don't call me Ma'am, Philip, call me Diana. Yes, I suppose I do to some extent, but I don't want to just carry on doing the sort of things I did while on Earth. I still want to help and care for people and show them that love is always there from someone, however dark your moment might be in your individual life. I am also growing as a person and I am spending much time in the wonderful halls of education and knowledge that we have here. You know, Philip, I wasn't that academically capable in my physical body and I often felt shy and embarrassed when dealing with people who were obviously far more intellectual than I was. I had always wished I'd had a better education than I did, and that is exactly what I am concentrating on doing here. It is a different sort of knowledge I strive for; it is the knowledge of understanding the more important things of helping people to care for and love each other. Do you know who is my great friend here?"

"No Diana, please tell me."

"Mother Teresa. She is a lovely little lady and we have so much in common. She and I are hoping very much to start a hospital on this side of existence for those who come over to us from your world who suffer from the awful conditions of AIDS and cancer. It is very much my wish to help nurse and guide these people in their transitional period as they come to us. It is also very much my wish to keep in touch with your world through people like yourself—genuine mediums—so that we may be able to bring our influence to bear, to care and love each other."

"You know, Diana, I have never met anyone who was so forgiving and understanding and caring as you were. Are you angry about those that were left behind such as Prince Charles, James Hewitt, and people of that nature?"

"No, not at all. I have moved on to something far higher now. But you know I never did have any bad feelings towards Charles. In many ways, he is a very good man and there will always remain a certain love between us, but we just had so little in common that perhaps our marriage was doomed to fail from the start. Then again, I am learning a thing over here called progression, which you already know about, don't you, Philip?"

"I hope so, Diana."

"Well, spending time with Charles was about my progression and gave me the opportunity to try to achieve the good things I tried to do, though I know I made many mistakes. I am sure James Hewitt was one of those mistakes, but part of that progression as well. I hold no malice towards him either. In fact, if you ever see him you may tell him that when he went into the little church and he said the words he did at the altar, they did reach me and I do accept what he said. He should be careful that people do not use him in the way he perhaps feels he used me. But basically, I have no regrets about my life in the body, and I am now looking forward to my life in spirit, still hoping to continue to help people."

"Okay, Diana, tell me more of your life in spirit."

"I have told you very much of what is happening already to me. At the moment it is very early days."

"It was a horrible accident that happened to you . . ."

"You did say accident, didn't you, Philip?"

"Yes, but whatever, it was an awful thing that happened to you, wasn't it?"

"It was. But there were those on this side who knew what would happen and that they would have to be ready to bring me over. My father was there, as I have told you, and I didn't have to spend too much time in hospital adjusting to my time here. Unfortunately, Dodi is still in a situation of readjusting, and I am spending much time in these hospital situations, especially with Mother Teresa. I do hope and pray that those who come over who have loved me and cared for me will believe that people such as myself and others will be waiting to show our gratitude and to welcome them to our world."

"What else are you doing, Diana?"

"Well, Philip, I always loved America, and though it was not publicly known, if things had been different I would have spent the second part of my life there. I have met many American people, film stars and politicians, actors and actresses, and they were friends. Those who had come here many years before me but still admired my work are now showing me and teaching me how to operate in that field as well. So there is a possibility that I will become an actress as well."

"My word, Diana, if you are going to organize your own hospital with Mother Teresa and become a film actress, you are going to be busy, aren't you? Do you think it is possible to do all those things at the same time?"

"As others will have told you, Philip, it is only really a matter of thinking of what you want to do and it is there for you; isn't it really? And that is what I am doing at the moment. Of course, it means I am far too busy to talk to you any longer, so I am going to leave it at that for now. But I know the other things I have told you about my life and that I have asked you to keep private, you will. I shall always help you whenever you ask me to. Good luck with the book. Bye for now."

CHAPTER 14

INTERVIEW WITH MAY THOMPSON

The story of May Thompson came by communication with me on May 16, 1998, at 7:30 P.M.:

May had been told by the "Big Boss," as she called him (what you and I might call God), that she had been chosen to put over the ordinary person's view of the spirit world so that I and others could give an explanation to those in our world of what it is like in the spirit life after death. May Thompson had worked in service for a very rich, aristocratic English family in middleclass Shropshire, from daybreak to dusk, skivvying at the beck and call of her masters. It was typical mid-aristocracy, people who considered May no more in the social strata than their horses. Indeed some of the family members would have treated the horses better!

Born the third daughter of nine children, at twelve she was sent into service (or slavery as she called it); by the age of fifteen she had passed to the higher life following acute appendicitis, operated on too late to save her. You would think she would be bitter about her life on this side but she told me, "Philip, I have learned so much. It was part of my progression. Only by suffering and seeing the wicked side of your world could I appreciate what I have here in the spirit world which is beautiful in every way."

"Okay then," I said, "tell me about it, May. How do you spend your time? Tell me every little detail."

"Well, first you must always remember that we do not follow time as you do. Just about anything I want would be here for me in the twinkling of a thought. For example, I never experienced sex in the body. I was not grown up enough for this and, of course, far too young, but I do enjoy the physical experience on this side."

"So you are telling me, May, that sex is possible in your world?"

"Oh, yes, indeed, My partner, Albert, and I simply merge. The very special experience similar to what people on Earth feel is there for us."

"Excuse me then, May, how can I put it without embarrassment, but do you actually copulate?"

"No, not actually because we do not have a physical body to do that, not in the way you mean. But we do sort of materialize and merge, perfectly blend if you like, a bit like oxygen and air. A very heightened sexual experience is there for us."

"Do all spirit people have relationships like these?"

"No. Actually, you will find that on this side of existence most people do not have a physical sex life, but it is possible. It just depends on the individual. If you didn't experience something like that in your physical life, as I didn't, of course it is important for you to experience it in this life. Everything is perfectly acceptable and understood on this side. It is basically what is right for you as an individual or couple, the way Albert and I are."

"There is another question I would like to ask then. Do you have night and day and working hours and sleeping hours as we do on Earth?"

"Yes, we do. We all have tasks to do, but the things we want to do are interesting. Of course, sleeping is a beautiful experience that is enjoyed when you are in the body and is something you would bring over with you and continue to do, but this is only in the first levels of existence before we progress to higher states where sleeping is not required."

"Tell me more about your life in spirit. Which level do you come from?"

"I am from level two, and this is the place that most people you would call real mediums in your world tune in to."

"Do you eat and drink?"

"We can, and anything I want would be there set before me. Beautiful, sumptuous food and wine as sweet as nectar are nothing more than a thought away. But for some time, Philip, I have not felt the need for such sustenance."

"So it's a choice?"

"Yes, that's right. We choose to have or not to have what we want. Of course, you should remember that on the first levels, they all eat and drink, many of them with great greed!"

"Let me ask you another question. Do you sleep in a bed in the manner we do on the Earth?"

"Yes. Again, if I choose to experience that it is there for me. I often sleep when I think of the evening hours that I spent in my little bed in my physical life. It was a time I loved when the hard toil of the day was behind me and all was still and quiet at the very top of the house I worked in. I sleep and remember, and all is very dark and peaceful for me here in this spirit world; but then after a while I awaken, think of daylight and the beautiful sunlight is there, and I am back on the vibration to do things in my daylight hours, as you call them."

"So what do you do then?"

"I am doing a lot of studying."

"What sort of things are you studying?"

"In the way many people are interested in the spirit world on your plane, I have an interest in the higher worlds. I hope one day to progress towards them, for I do not think I want to come back to your world to gain experience."

"So people can do that?"

"Oh, yes, of course you can choose to come back if you want to. Of course, you have to have the permission of the Higher Ones to do so and show that you have a need to learn to progress. But that is not the way for me, I don't think. Therefore, I am studying in a way similar to the way you would on Earth for your degrees and various other examinations."

"So you know about these things then. You are aware of our world as well."

"Oh, yes, we have wonderful mediums on our side that are just like yours who tell us about your world. You and the wonderful Hans Holzer are the first ones to really try to get this understanding for people in your world, but there are people on this side who have related the experiences of your world and what is happening today, many, many times."

"So how did you get through to me today then? Is there a medium that works between you and me, or is this imagination on my part, or are you really speaking to me?"

"Well, let me put it this way to you. You are a very special medium and anything is possible with a special medium. Ask Hans Holzer about these things. Maybe he can explain the way you are more easily than you can yourself!"

"Okay, then, May, I will do that. You told me that you met Albert when you were in the spirit world rather than the way others come over and reunite with loved ones, as others have told me. So is it possible to meet and fall in love in the spirit world?"

"Oh, yes, of course. We fall in love and out of love, much the same as you do in your world, for we still retain all our emotions and, in truth, are not that much wiser than you are. Indeed, many people seem to think that by communicating with ordinary people in our world we can give you wonderful advice and put you forward to live and move forward in your own world in a more sensible way, but that is not true. We have the same emotional difficulties on this second level of experience of the Higher Life as you do in your first level, although when you are advised from the higher levels, the way some mediums are, then this can be accepted as very fine guidance."

"Tell me something then. I know this may seem a funny question, but who are the bosses in your world? Who is in charge? Who tells people what they can and cannot do?"

"Okay, I will try to explain that to you. There are those in your world who speak of guides and have tuned into the Ancient Ones of great wisdom. These are the ones who govern our world even more closely than they do in yours, for though anything is possible with just thinking of it in our world, we have progressed slightly and tend not to make the same mistakes as we did in our physical body. It is our belief that this is because we are closer to these guides that you talk of than you are. These are what you would term the 'bosses,' and they come down and visit our level from the higher realms."

"What sort of people are they?"

"Well, they are people who would have, perhaps, been great religious leaders and men and women of peace who helped to make your world progress, such as Mahatma Gandhi, presidents such as John F. Kennedy and Abraham Lincoln. But you must understand I am only giving you a small number of examples. You must not take these as hard facts for it is not possible for me to tell you of these guides. Certainly these people join with us to help us decide when it is time to come back and experience life on the Earth plane, and we certainly have the free choice to do so. We also have to make out a case for needing to learn, and we make this progression to these higher guides or bosses. That is what you are asking me about, isn't it, Philip?"

"Yes, I suppose so, May. Yes, I suppose it is. Do you have any health problems, and are there hospitals in your world?"

"Yes, we have many hospitals, and when people first come over to this level of experience, they are often poorly and need to spend time recuperating. Our hospitals are not like yours though, for we have no people who have long-lasting illness, or die, to use that word that we don't like to say!"

"One final question. How do you find loved ones in the spirit world who have come over from the physical plane? Is it easy to do or is it difficult?"

"Well, Philip, you have been told by many people that when you pass from your world there is always someone to take you over to our side and introduce you to those close to you and who will maybe work with you in the future. Therefore, it is as simple as that, really. There is always someone to introduce you to your loved ones when you come over."

"What about great grandparents and people like that whom we may have had an interest in through tracing our ancestors?"

"It is very likely that they will be aware of the interest that you have shown in them and are waiting just as eagerly to meet you. But do remember that some of them lived maybe hundreds of years ago in your understanding of time, and they may have progressed to either higher levels or have come back to the physical plane and are living lives in your world now!"

"Yes, that's an interesting point. So what happens to the widower who has come over to your world and finds their partner is not there? How are they consoled?"

"Philip, many have explained to you that anything you wish to sense—your heart's desire—would be there for you, so I don't really feel I need to explain that again. Whatever you want or desire will be there for you."

"But it's not real then is it?"

"Reality is whatever you are part of."

"This is difficult to understand and accept."

"I am doing my best for you, but these are very complex things you are asking me and as a simple woman I am trying to explain them in simple terms."

"Yes, I realize that, May. I didn't mean to be rude and I really am very grateful to you."

"Not at all. It is a pleasure to communicate with you, but it is time for me to go now."

"May, there are so many more things I would like to ask you."

"Yes, I know, but I have given you all the information there is to give. Therefore, I will wish you every happiness in your life and success with all the good things you do. Goodbye for now."

CHAPTER 15

MICHAEL'S COMMUNICATION

Michael made contact with me on June 3, 1998, at 4:45 P.M., on what was a very busy day for me. My wife and I were to attend a family party to celebrate our twenty-fifth wedding anniversary, but Michael felt his message was urgent, that he needed it to get through to me that day, and that it was important I write it down for the book. It is perhaps more academic than some of the communications I have been given and perhaps for some it will prove very important.

He started off by telling me about our world. "Philip, let me tell you one fact. Your planet Earth is the most wonderful, indeed the most beautiful in the universe as you know it, and it has more physical beauty than any other planet. In truth, my son, nothing in the existence of human consciousness is more beautiful than your planet Earth. That is why it attracts so many souls and spirit essences, which, once they have visited your place, wish to come back again and again. It has so many positive and negative aspects that more can be learned there than anywhere else in existence, perhaps with the exception of the spirit world. God created Earth to be a paradise and it will become a paradise again. It is important for those on Earth, though, to understand that they are not alone and that there is no end to life, and that for everything you sow, so shall you reap. But enough of what you might call religious overtones for that is not what I am about at all."

"Michael, I would like to ask you a question. You know I have been very successful in my career as a medium and have made predictions that some people have described as amazing but to me have seemed quite natural. How do I manage to do this, yet on occasions get things wrong?"

"That is an interesting point, Philip. As always, you have shown yourself to be astute and in tune with us on this side. I tell you in truth, my son, I am one of those people who has always influenced you and given you this ability. This is one of the pathways I have chosen in my everyday life, to work with people like you on Earth; and, indeed, Philip, there are eight others who are very similar to you, and one day you will all join together and help your world in its darkest hour."

"What do mean, the world's darkest hour, Michael?"

"That is not something you need to know about at the moment, Philip, for that is part of your future. But I will tell you this: I have a role amongst a group of other people on this side of existence that means I can be anywhere at any time, past, present, or future, and it is my group that have told you things."

"But Michael if you can be in the future then you would positively know what is going to happen and I would never get anything wrong. Please explain things to me more clearly."

"I will try, Philip, and although your gift is great there are some things you will not be able to understand. As a group, when we sit together in the Great Circle, your world underneath us is clearly in view but there are also hills and other obstacles which you will never be aware of in your physical being; but we can see through those obstacles. This represents the past and what it was like on the Other Side of those obstacles for we have been there and seen these things for ourselves. In front, we see other obstacles, but we do not see behind them, only around them. I emphasize this, Philip: *only around them.*

"When you go round an obstacle you always see several pathways that leads to an ending; the choice is always there. What I am saying to you is that not only one future lies before your people, but many futures. This is there to involve your free will and if you were to know more explicitly what the future holds as we do then we would become more instrumental in your planet's evolvement, and your free will would then have been removed. This would affect progress for all of you.

"As an example think of the Western world that you live in and remember the decade of the Sixties. If the great one, Kennedy, had not been there for your Western world, then your future would not have come forward and progressed into the new age that you have now. Indeed, the future of your world would have been very changed; but if Kennedy had not been there, then, of course, another would have been ready to step forward to take you in another direction."

"You are confusing me, Michael. This doesn't explain to me how I can see the future in the way I do."

"I understand, Philip, that this is not the perfect explanation for you but there is not another way for me to make it any more simple for you. But understand this: my group and I do not exactly pre-set your future, although, basically, it is set before you and people such as yourself can be given glimpses of that future. It is as simple as that and I can tell you no more."

"May I ask you one final question on this subject then?"

"You may."

"Many of the mystics and psychics predict that the world will come to an end and that we are approaching that time. Is this so?"

"There is one matter for which I will give you guarantees for the future of your wonderful planet, Philip. That is, my group and those above me will never allow the total decimation of your planet, whichever pathway you take to your future. We would intervene at that time if your people were to threaten its very existence."

"Thank God for that, Michael!"

"Thank yourselves for that, Philip!"

"Michael, please don't think I am being rude in what I am going to say to you now but a lot of the information I am getting from you is wonderful but it's not really what Hans wants for our book. He wants to know what it is like in the spirit realms, you know, everyday happenings, that kind of thing. So without sounding rude, can I ask you what you do?"

"You make me laugh. We are well aware of brother Hans who has always wanted to know much of these realms and has prayed for many moons for someone like you to come into his friendship circle who could tell him. But in truth, not even he, who has given so much to spirit, can know everything. But I will explain a little to you about who and what I am and what the realms you ask of are like. My life, as you put it, revolves around working with eight or nine other people. Our essence is only energy and we have no physical body at all. We look over and guide all but are particularly interested in your planet Earth, although there are many other mansions that are certainly of interest to us. In the spirit realms there are seven levels of existence. Each is part of an overall consciousness that has an interest in the level below it, and from each level physical people are reincarnated upon your place of being where you are now, Earth. We are on the highest but one level and are greatly evolved and have a responsibility to oversee the whole of the universes. This is my everyday work that you inquire of, Philip, and unfortunately, neither you nor Hans at the moment will be able to comprehend it, let alone your readers!"

"Okay, then, Michael, do you live in a place that has buildings, cities and industry?"

"On some of the levels of course we do, and you will have been told by others that what they wish to be there will be there for them. But on the higher levels, such as my group, we are like a small tribe, collectively working together in everyday existence, like an extended Earth family, if you like. We have no cities or towns and live in one place a bit like a great temple which has within it many crystals that create energy and light. Yes, that is a very good way to explain to you what it is like. But I must tell you we are operating at very high consciousness levels, and although we are individual and singular, in many ways we merge and act as one in perfect attunement."

"You know, Michael, you're still not really telling me exactly what you do in your everyday work in the spirit world or for Earth."

"Philip, do not think that Earth or the spirit world are the only places where my work is done. Remember that Earth is not the only occupied life planet."

"What are you telling me, Michael—that there is life on other planets and that you can communicate with them?"

"I'm not telling you anything on that subject; but Earth is by no means the only planet that we, on the higher levels of the spirit world, are interested in. You must draw your own conclusions from that comment. Let me take you back to where you asked me what my work is. It is not a very good word that you used, 'work,' for I above, like you below, choose to do what I wish to do. Service might be a better word than work even though it is partly progression, for we are all given free will by the Creator to do whatever we wish, wherever we are. Even angels are faced with the same choices that you as physical beings are faced with. We are all on a progression pathway. Remember, wherever you are, Philip, that all people have cosmic meaning in the life they live. Understand me, Philip, when I say to you that those who have come back from the spirit realms to serve on Earth make that decision before that particular lifetime."

"May I ask you a question, Michael? Why is it that when people look at past lives, or are hypnotically regressed or something of that nature, they often say they have come back and lived lives together? Is that true?"

"Of course it is true, and that would have been your and their decision."

"Okay, so if you have the memories of past lives, how is it that you cannot retrieve experiences of the spirit in memory?"

"That happens because there is a subconscious block that has to be placed for you to come back and learn and progress further. It is not for you to remember the past that you shared with others in spirit."

"Michael, I know this will probably make you angry, but, again, can I ask you about what your life is in the world you live in, and who you are, and what you do, as this is what we are trying to get this book together for."

"Yes, you do make me angry, Philip, because what I am

telling you is more important, but I will answer some of your points. I am servant of the one you would call God, part of an angelic group of nine individuals collectively come together in mind. Of course, at one time there were ten of us, but that is another story!"

"So who is your boss then? Who do you represent?"

"The force that is way above both you and me, Philip, that commands, loves and directs all; yet for all that, connects with all, is totally part of you and me, and, indeed, the whole universe and can only be described in one word. You ask who is my boss—I say to you One."

"Let me ask you something. There are people who will say to you that if we carry on after our physical death, why do we have the need for doctors and nurses in this world, or the gifted healers who heal the sick?"

"There is a simple answer to that. The importance of having the physical body being healed and returned to natural balance is quite simply so that the spirit within can fulfill its purpose and receive its learning time on your Earth plane; basically to go on as long as is required in your world. Sometimes your physical bodies are old and weak and we give you the healing to carry on and continue doing and following the purpose."

"Do you have a female friend, a girlfriend, or a wife?"

"No, on my level gender does not exist. I have however both a male and female side present in my energy source though I have progressed on from what you would call sexuality and this is no longer part of my existence."

"If you are part of a group of angels, Michael, who operate on the highest level, who is your big boss?"

"That's a funny question, Philip. All of us are part of the big boss, as you call it. With progress, collectively, eventually we become one, what you would call God; but remember that you, also, and even those who have very little spirituality in your world are still on that ultimate progression to becoming One."

"So your work is a bit like a board of directors then?"

"From your physical levels of understanding I can see how

you put that, Philip, and I suppose in a way that would be so. But do remember what I have told you, for those below us all have free will and progression is always part of free will. In truth, Philip, without questioning me, we on this level are also much involved in mediumship between the seven worlds. We, the angels, link with you on Earth and assist the communications between you and your loved ones on level two and three and are always trying to protect you from wicked influences that come out and surround you in your world from level one."

"Are there mediums on all levels then, between different existences, and how are they chosen?"

"We, the angels, choose them, and, yes, there are some people who interact between the higher levels in an upward way; but it is important for you to know communication between your world, Earth, and the spirit levels you mediate with is on the first three levels. Those in the first three levels of existence on this side have no need for a medium, for they use the medium in your world to communicate with whom they wish to speak to on your plane. Also, remember very clearly, Philip, that no medium, whatever their claims in your world, can ever contact specific individuals in the spirit world. It is always the other way round. Spirit contacts the medium and asks for messages to be passed on to those they feel are in need of help and guidance. However, there are some mediums, no more than ten are incarnated at the moment in the whole of your world, who can facilitate communication between all levels of spirit existence, right up to the very highest existence. In the past such people were called prophets and have guided and helped your world. Today, many charlatans exist who pretend to be mediums and psychics, and those you would call prophets today are not recognized except by those with a great deal of experience and spiritual knowledge."

"So let me get this clear in conclusion, Michael. You are an angel?"

"Yes!"

"You work with other angels to jointly govern all existence?"

"Yes!"

"You are especially designated the role of allowing mediumship between the levels?"

"No! Wrong! That is only a part of my work. I also influence and advise those below on rebirth, spiritual growth, and progression. This is a collective work that is done between all of us higher, advanced souls, and is given to benefit and influence all, especially to all those in the levels below us."

"Again, let me get this clear then, Michael, your boss is ultimately God?"

"Yes, Philip, that is basically accurate, but remember we are all sons and daughters of God, and that ultimately progress leads to oneness. What you know and call God is the completeness, the ultimate end of the pathway, the final finished object of all of us. All of us have God, or the Son of God if you like, within, and I cannot think of a better time to finish my communication with you, Philip, than now. Thank you."

"No, Michael, thank you very much indeed. Goodbye!"

CHAPTER 16

ROSEMARY AND LARRY VISIT THE THEATER AND LIBRARY

This communication was given to me from Rosemary and Larry on June 4, 1998, at 7:30 P.M., so that people living in our world would have an understanding of how you can still carry on your life visiting the places you enjoy in the spirit world.

Rosemary and Larry were reunited in the spirit world after being together for many years in the body. Rosemary had passed over some years after Larry, at the age of eighty-five, whereas Larry had gone over much sooner, when he was fifty-two. But now both of them were in their prime, perhaps twenty-five or twenty-six, very much as they were when they were together in the body and so much in love. Indeed, Larry always prided himself on how smart he looked in his RAF uniform, which certainly was something he couldn't have worn in the last five years of his life when he gained a lot of weight before having the heart attack which made him pass to the higher levels.

In the spirit world, Rosemary always wore a very smart blue suit, similar to the one she wore when in the body, and everyone remarked on how much she looked like Betty Grable, the film star who had been very much admired by people between the two world wars.

Rosemary and Larry told me how impressed they had

been by a person they called a Wise One who had helped them when Rosemary came over to the spirit world. They told me how they admired everything this person had taught them, and they told me of the things that were available to them and how so much of the wonderful things they had enjoyed in the physical world and had missed so much, especially Rosemary in her latter years, were now there for them in the spirit world. They told me they had visited the theater and library in the spirit world.

Rosemary told me that one day she was speaking to this great guide when she stopped him for a moment and told him she had heard that many people were attending a theater show that evening. She had asked the guide if it would be possible that Larry and she could go to such an event. Apparently the guide had smiled and told her of course it was possible, and, indeed, that evening they found themselves part of what seemed a very long queue of young, vibrant people walking through beautiful hills of green up to a place they called the theater. It would seem that thousands of people were thronging there to hear a concert by Rosemary's absolute favorite artist, Frank Sinatra, who apparently had only just come over to the spirit world about a week before, and yet was so perfectly in balance with his progression that he had immediately agreed to give a performance to his thousands of fans in the spirit world.

Upon arrival at the theater, which Rosemary thought was very much like the Roman amphitheaters she had seen in films such as *Ben Hur*, she saw that in the middle was a small spotlighted area where the star was to perform. Rosemary noticed there were no seats. Larry smiled and a couple who were standing beside them laughed and told Rosemary that in spirit she would not get physically tired as she did in the body and would have no need of a seat. Thousands of people were coming to the amphitheater from all directions and were standing around, when suddenly into the middle of the theater stepped the great Frank Sinatra. Rosemary turned to Larry and commented on the great number of people who had arrived and that there were no microphones.

"How will anyone hear Frank?" she asked. "We are so far back, we certainly won't be able to hear!"

"Rosemary, there are even people outside this theater who will hear Mr. Sinatra perfectly clearly!" Larry answered with a smile.

They turned again to the center of the amphitheater and saw the entry of the musicians. Rosemary also noticed Sammy Davis, Jr., someone else she admired greatly, in the center of the theater hugging and caressing Frank Sinatra and introducing him to many people.

"Oh, if only I could meet him!" she exclaimed,

"You can," answered Larry, "but let that wait for a little time. Remember this gentleman has only just come over to this side and has thousands of fans who are desperate to hear and see him."

"Like me!" replied Rosemary.

At that moment the amphitheater fell silent. Mr. Sinatra introduced himself in much the same way as he would have done in shows on Earth and then immediately opened his concert with the old favorite, "My Way." All the people clapped and cheered with approval. The musicians and orchestra were wonderfully talented, but a number of the instruments, although very similar to those used on Earth, like double bass, cello, guitar, clarinet, and bass, stood out more than the others. Some instruments were very different and had very different sounds which could only be described as spiritual and beautiful. There was also an instrument which, when played, was beautifully clear and high-pitched. Larry explained that this was very similar to the synthesizer used on Earth, but was more advanced, capable of producing anything.

"Shh!" said Rosemary. "I'm listening to Frank."

"I'm sorry," said Larry, smiling at his beloved wife.

In a matter of seconds, it became clear to Rosemary that the rest of the orchestra would support this wonderful instrument that was like a synthesizer and that was responsible for most of the music that supported Mr. Sinatra. Of course, Rosemary had never known Frank Sinatra in the body, but apparently quite early in his career he had had a problem with his throat, and although the general public was never to know this, he never sang as well again as he had in his thirties. Now that voice was as good, as clear, and as perfect as ever. Rosemary and Larry were captivated by the performance.

Rosemary turned to Larry and said, "How can he perform like that? He must have had no time to practice with these people or to rehearse!"

"Rosemary, in the spirit world, you need no practice or set programs. You do not need to rehearse at all. Just a wish to do the thing and it is there for you. Do you remember how it was always my ambition to play music, the piano or guitar?"

"I do, Larry, but you were tone deaf!"

"I'll give you a surprise then. I play piano very well and I am also mastering the guitar."

"No! Surely not," she replied.

"Rosemary, anything is possible in the spirit world. Just what you want is there for you."

Rosemary was very surprised to see that all the musicians in the orchestra were famous people. Larry explained to her that this was often the case, that many of the great musicians and performers would come together and give examples of their work in performances such as the couple were witnessing on this particular evening. Eventually Frank Sinatra's performance came to an end, and at this stage the man who had played the synthesizer took over and led the orchestra, starting off with what seemed like a very easily remembered collection of notes. In a flash Rosemary remembered what it was. It was the music she had heard in Steven Spielberg's film, *Close Encounters of the Third Kind*: da-da-da-da-da!

She looked at Larry and smiled, "I always loved that you know. There always seemed to be something special about that film for me."

"Why do you think he is playing it, Rosemary? I requested it for you."

There were dancers in the middle of the theater, and as the music changed and the tempo increased and moved quickly from different keys, yet in perfect balance, so the dancers moved and swayed in perfect harmony. It was the most beautiful example of color and dance you could imagine, and, as Rosemary put it, no words could describe it. The dancers moved in incredible movements, their beautiful white robes flowing around them in perfect attunement with the beautiful, individual melodies the synthesizer played. The music and the dancing carried on for what seemed two or three hours, but to Rosemary, who was new to the spirit world, this was hard to understand. To Larry, it was simply that the concert would last as long as they wished it to, as long as it gave them exquisite pleasure.

They were exalted and lifted by the spirit of the music, but eventually it was time for the couple to make their way home. In a natural, perfect procession, they joined many other thousands of people who seemed to leave the amphitheater behind, smiling at each other, friendly, happy, making their way back through the hills to the place that Rosemary and Larry would share as their home in their spirit life. Completely happy and so very uplifted, Rosemary and Larry stopped for a short while to look at the many beautiful plants and flowers in the hedgerows and nearby places. These were beautiful spirit flowers which have such wonderful colors and fragrances that it cannot be described except to say that they presented a beauty beyond comprehension on Earth.

About half way back from the theater Rosemary noticed a breathtaking crystal building of great size and of unusual shapes but similar in some aspects to the buildings of Egypt, especially the pyramids and Sphinx which she had found so beautiful on her trips to Egypt with her husband during their physical life. Walking to one building, which looked very much like a glass pyramid, she looked inside and noticed that it was a library. The walls were covered in a substance that looked much like amber on one wall and crystal amethyst on another; another wall glittered with gold. The building seemed to have the most wonderful atmosphere of peace and relaxation and quickly communicated to Rosemary that here was a place of great wisdom.

But this library, Rosemary thought, held wisdom she

would never be able to understand in the physical world. Inside, the library seemed much bigger than on the outside, and peering in as far as she could see, even in this first entrance hall she saw row after row of books. Beautiful books bound in beautiful materials. They were greeted by what must have been a librarian, a tall, elegant young lady with a wonderfully pleasing and kindly face and lovely personality. At the same time, despite her youth and beauty, she was obviously a person who exuded a great understanding and knowledge.

"Just pick whichever book you are drawn to," she said. "You will find in this place the books will often draw you and that many things you need to know and understand in this existence will be presented to help you. But I would like to suggest, Rosemary, that you take these three or four books in particular that I have chosen for you and spend a little time reading them. If you enjoy them I am sure they will be of benefit to you. One is a book that explains how human beings have progressed and developed, and chosen to progress, and how they live many lives in the physical world; and, indeed, it discusses the meaning of coming to the spirit world. I shall not refer you to this book again but I will allow you to keep the book if you wish to use it as a source of reference for your progression in the future. The other books you find will have much guidance, and you should see them basically as books that introduce you to a new place of wonderful enjoyment, much the same as a guide book for when you visit somewhere on your holidays on Earth. I have had that same experience of the Earth plane as you have." Rosemary thanked her, took the books, and selected a few more she felt drawn to, as the librarian had suggested she could.

When Rosemary and Larry finally got home, they sat together and held hands for a while, then examined the books Rosemary had chosen. She also spent time running her hands over the wonderful covers trying to associate herself with the materials they were made from, appreciating their wonderful craftsmanship. The feeling she had as she touched them was that they were not just books produced to make profits, but were part of her own spiritual pathway.

Larry, as if telepathically attuning to his wife, said, "You are right, that is exactly what they are. But they don't all have to be like that as there are also here the kinds of books you would have loved to read and enjoy in your earthly existence. Anything you want is there for you, whether it be a romantic novel or an academic manual."

Rosemary looked at her husband and smiled. "That sounds wonderful. The trouble is these books are so beautiful that I feel almost ashamed to say that I shall miss my paperbacks."

"If it's paperbacks you want, they will be at the library for you just the same as on Earth!" he replied. "Anything you want, my darling, is there for you."

Rosemary and Larry looked at one another and decided that for this evening it would not be books that would bring them the great pleasure they had in their earthly lives together, but the pleasure of each other; their memories of a wonderful evening at the theater, a surprise visit to a library, and their perfect happiness in each other's company.

CHAPTER 17

THE SPIRIT JOHN AND PHILIP HAVE A QUESTION-AND-ANSWER SESSION

For this particular session which took place on June 7, 1998, at 6:45 P.M., it was arranged that I would sit with a group of my students, whom I train and develop into professional and proficient mediums, in a meditative session where they would all send power towards me, and I would attempt to make myself available to the spirit world. We hoped we would be blessed with John's company, a spirit who has worked with me many times, and that he would come through and speak to us so that these experienced students would have the opportunity to ask John questions regarding the spirit world. I would make it clear through my mediumship with John that if it was his agreement, this material could be used for the book. These are some of the questions put to John by the students:

Question: "John, if the first level is where everyone goes initially, including criminals, murderers, and pedophiles, does this mean normal people have to mix with them?"

Answer: "Your information is flawed, my child. Very few people, except the very wicked, like those you have described, go to the first level. Most people you call 'normal,' who live good everyday lives, go to the second level of existence.

There, people like my friend, Philip, communicate and link with people such as yourself and your loved ones. I would warn you not to judge, for people such as you have outlined must progress eventually, perhaps through a rebirth in your world, to come back and reach a stage of being acceptable spirit people in that second level of existence. Always remember what that wise one who came among you said: 'Let he who is without sin throw the first stone.'"

Question: "What about eating meat—is that acceptable, and what happens to the animals, to their spirit or essence after we have eaten them?"

Answer: "You must understand that all things progress, all things come into the spirit world. However, when their time comes to an end in your world, their progression is different to yours. As for eating flesh, it is very much for individuals to decide what is right and wrong for them, for it is part of their progression. If you feel you must eat meat, then you must; it is part of your pathway. Perhaps one of the best ways to see that pathway more clearly and to decide what is right or wrong for you as an individual is, if you have a pet, a favorite cat or dog, to think what would your inner feeling be about killing that creature, cooking it, and then eating it? For that is an animal surely no different from the animals of the forest; but you are given free will to decide upon these things yourself. In truth there is no judgement of you. You have asked me as well, where do these animals progress to? Do they come to the spirit world the way that you do? In some instances they do, for if you wish those loved pets or beautiful animals to be part of your existence in the spirit world when you come forth, then they will surely be there. In truth, many of them are not of such essence and several animals may be part of an overall progression upwards. Indeed, in the truth of reincarnation, they are lesser than your spirit which is great."

Question: "Where do the little babies go that are terminated, or who are stillborn, or who are few in years when they pass away?"

Answer: "Nothing 'passes away,' my child. These little ones that you speak of are certainly from the kingdom I come from, without sin and pure, and very close to those you would call guides in your world. Very often it is difficult for the mother in your world who loses a little baby or makes the decision to terminate a child, which is often later regretted, to accept that is the end of it. Indeed, it is not the end of it. Did not that woman at some time have a mother or grandmother whom she loved, or even maybe an older lady who showed her great affection in her life? In truth, know that the little children you speak of will be drawn to such as these and will be kept in the love of their arms.

"Also, there are times in your world when little children pass over to us following awful and terrible deaths about which you have no comprehension as to why they should suffer in such a dreadful way. I will tell you that these are the specially chosen ones who have made much progression from other lives and who return quickly to a higher, more beautiful world in spirit. For every second they have suffered in their little lives on Earth, they will spend hours and days in bliss in the spirit realms, for they are the little diamonds and stars that shine brighter than anything you know in your world. Know, also, they are aware of their parents and will visit via mediums or on your own vibration, and are always there loving you the way any child in your physical life does."

Question: "John, what about the person who over-indulges in whatever he or she desires? For example, over-eating. Is that possible in your world? Or someone who has sex without love with many partners, and things of that nature?"

Answer: "Your question is a strange one. Do you mean over-eating in your physical body? For in truth, unless it is something you greatly enjoyed in the physical, you will have no real need to eat in my world; though, of course, as others will have told you, if it is something that was important and pleasurable to you then that will be there for you. Also, your question about sex with many partners is a difficult one to answer. Do you mean as in your physical world? For if that was something you did in the physical world, generally it would be a person searching for affection who has not had the true love of a mother or father and who finds comfort in the arms of many people even though they may not show the love that is searched for.

"In my world we would pity that person and not be judgmental, and I would have to say to you that in my world if you wished to eat to excess it would be there for you if it was what you needed. Even sex is possible and with many partners if that was what you wished, though not exactly in the way you know it; it would be more a union of mind or a blending, if you like. There are certainly those who would come over with the same desires and wishes who would accommodate individuals with those requirements. But in truth it would show that you had not made the progress that you would need to move upwards and onwards, for true love with many partners is unusual, and sex without love would never satisfy the deep inner spiritual needs."

Question: "Do people who have done very bad things get an actual punishment or are they allowed to think what they want and immediately have it?"

Answer: "The answer to that, my dear, is yes. They would, but these are the people, generally, who have very much to learn. The very bad people would go to that first level of existence between your world and the second level of existence where, I can promise you, most of the people you love exist. The people on that second level are always hopeful that they can reach out and help those on level one, hopefully to change their attitudes, wants, and needs to become more developed and good people. No one is ever rejected, and it is always hoped that they can change and find goodness within themselves. Their punishment would be to stay the person they are and not progress. I must say to you, my child, that of course they are allowed free will, and if the things they want bring them pleasure it is possible for them to bring those things into their vibration and satisfy their needs. Always be well protected psychically and allow the power of prayer to protect you from people such as these on this first level of existence. It is also a fact that often they draw close to the Earth plane and people who are not experienced but who have some slight mediumistic ability can attract these people through the use of planchettes, Ouija boards, and the like; and it may well be that I say to you that the voyeur, the Peeping Tom, and the rapist would not change immediately, and that very lack of change that remains with them is a great punishment indeed."

Question: "What about people who do not want to be guided on the right path and who enjoyed bad and evil things in their life? Is it not true, John, that our personalities are not supposed to be that different when we pass over?"

Answer: "Yes, this is indeed true. When you first pass to the spirit existence, you are very much the same as when you were in the body. I have spoken to you of free will. If these people choose not to be guided then they still have free will in the first levels of existence. I thought I had made it very clear that the very evil people of your world pass to a first level of existence which is much closer, unfortunately, to your world than to the one we exist in. When people speak of earthbound spirits or ghosts that frighten people, generally it is this place that they come from, this first level.

"However, I have often laughed with my medium, Philip, when he tells me of his mother, a truly great servant of spirit, who always told people, 'Never think that your partner or friend becomes an angel just because they have passed to the spirit world. They are much the same as when they were on Earth, and if they were characters that you could only describe as incorrigible rogues, then incorrigible rogues they will be as they first progress to the Other Side.' But a 'character' or 'incorrigible rogue' is not the same as evil. Do you understand what I am saying to you?"

Question: "How are these people who are evil punished? How are the people who have had dreadful crimes committed against them avenged?"

Answer: "I do not have the time to completely go over the same things I have told you several times. Their punishment is in their lack of progression. Vengeance is meted out and decided by the ones from the very highest levels, but sometimes to have crimes committed against you, or evil perpetrated upon you is part of your progression. For perhaps at some time in another life you have been such as this yourself, and how would you ever learn the wrongness of these things if it didn't happen to yourself in the physical? 'As you sow, so shall you reap.' Real learning is only ever really experienced by feeling the crime or the pain for yourself. This again is part of progress and progression, and vengeance is our domain, not yours."

Question: "How are the child murderers and molesters punished? Surely there must be a punishment for people such as these who offend against little children?"

Answer: "It is true. Such people as these are pure evil and offend against those who truly are the Light of the Kingdom of Heaven in its highest order; but everything has a way of coming round. Maybe such a poor and unfortunate child who suffers a horrendous crime, would be so especially gifted in understanding he could help little children who have to suffer such abuse in the physical world and also help them when they first come to us. The punishment of the offenders: you have asked so many times to explain punishment and I have said before almost certainly these people would go to the first level of existence, which is punishment enough. They would need many new lives in your world to progress and they would find it exceedingly difficult to progress to higher levels in our world. This would be their punishment."

Question: "If the existence in your world goes on forever and is infinite and we do not have to strive in any way to do the things we want, as others from your world have told us, and we just think about it and it is there, then does it not become a very boring, tiresome existence with people thinking this is going to go on forever and ever?"

Answer: "That is a good question but I tell you in truth, my child, you would not make progression to the levels of existence on a higher plane until you had the ability to appreciate and deserve such an existence. It is such a beautiful place that I can promise you that for not one second in your Earth time would you describe it as boring. Also remember that you would still be studying and progressing to move towards higher levels of consciousness."

Question: "Over there, do we wear clothes? Do we need to? Are our bodies visible to everyone? Are they the same? Do they feel the same? How is it possible to create everything with just our minds?"

Answer: "It was my understanding from my medium, Philip, that I would communicate with you tonight to answer individual questions, but you immediately present six to me. But I will strive to answer them for you. In truth, I think the world you think of is the second level of existence. Most people who exist on that level do wear clothes in much the same way they did on Earth, though if you did not wish to wear clothes and you felt comfortable with it then that would be perfectly acceptable. Yes, your body in that existence is visible and can be seen by everyone else. No, your body will not be the same as your body on Earth, but the touch, the texture, and feel would be the same as it had been on Earth. You ask if everything is created with our minds. My friend, the very universe exists because it has been created by a higher consciousness and mind."

Question: "Everyone has different ideas about what they like, so if we live with others how do we all agree about what surrounds us and what should be there?"

Answer: "Do you not have the same complexities in your present existence but do you not somehow agree amongst yourselves about the way things will be? There are people who find it important that a thing is presented in a specific way; for others this is not so important. But I tell you this, though it will be hard for you to understand: whatever you wish to have around you as an individual, as I and others have already told you, it will always be there."

Question: "Do objects feel solid?"

Answer: "Ah! That is a tiresome question. As I have told you many times, everything is exactly as you would wish it to be."

Question: "Is there a standard place that everyone sees and then we add to it ourselves? What is it like initially?"

Answer: "The realms of the spirit are the realms of the spirit and are as they are, as is the place you exist in. Do you not contribute to the beauty of your world? Do you not contribute to its pollution? The green planet that you live upon is very beautiful. The spirit world is the place of your dreams, initially, and it is fair to say that you contribute to its continuing beauty when you come to us."

Question: "What about the evil things people do—things that are unthinkable to the normal mind? Where do these ideas and actions come from? Is the force that makes them do these things a paranormal source, or is there an error in brain function? What causes it?"

Answer: "Your question, my friend, is a good question but belongs more to your world, or really at the very furthest extension to the first level of existence that I have spoken to you about. It is true there are those in your world who would attune to these people and beings on the first level of existence, and enjoy being part of those evil doings, for there is an evil within themselves and evil will always attract evil. However, you ask if someone with a brain dysfunction causes them to act inappropriately and not operate within the standards of what normal people would expect. These people are to be pitied, and when they come over to our existence, they come to the second level of existence and are put in places of rest, and hospitals where they are balanced and brought back into the community ready for rebirth in your world. Or they spend time in the spirit world to progress."

Question: "Why are some people saintly and some people devilish, apparently even in the spirit world?"

Answer: "All beings are given free will to choose pathways.

There are pathways of goodness and pathways of evil, in your world and in ours, though I tell you in truth, my friend, there are few that are saints and there are few that are devils."

Question: "Are these people who are bad, just basically bad with no excuses? Is it just the way they are?"

Answer: "Yes, this is so, but even for these there is always a possibility there for them to learn to progress."

Question: "Do people from, say, two hundred years ago adapt to modern times or do they stay locked in their own era in the spirit world?"

Answer: "Remember that many souls return to your world to live further lives and make progress and improve themselves and that many souls will have made progression upwards to higher levels of existence and wish to help and guide those below. It is true there are many who have lived in your world thousands of years ago, not just hundreds, who are very happy to progress on the second or third level of existence. Their world often is for them as it was in their earthly bodies. But there are also many who wish to progress and live in a future existence far in advance of the way you live. Many who live in your world have egos, and when they make wonderful inventions they think these are entirely from their own minds, but they are often influenced by a great scientist who has gone many years before. Do you think the minds of people like Newton, da Vinci, and Einstein would stay locked in their own times? I can tell you this is not so."

Question: "What is the point of all these different lives and existences?"

Answer: "Your question is silly and stupid, but I will answer it! From the tiniest life form to the Godhead, everything leads to progression. Many in your world seem to think the same thing, 'What is the point of it all?' and commit the awful act of suicide. I tell you in honesty, my friend, it is an act that is always regretted although suicides are never sent to the places that traditional religions say they are. Indeed, they are taken into our healing sanctuaries and brought into balance, but much is lost in the experience that would have been if they had lived out their life on Earth. Life is for living and learning and that is the point of it all."

Question: "What other kinds of communication are there? Is it possible to communicate with other forms of life, for example, with extraterrestrial aliens and things of that nature?"

Answer: "Yes, of course, and many in your world do for there are many places in your universe that support life as you know it, and there are many other universes where life exists, including beings who are very similar to yourself on the blue planet. But these are not the realms of the spirit world, and are of a dimension that is actually quite close to your world, but one exceedingly difficult to be aware of even for the greatest of your mediums."

Question: "Would you explain more of this?"

Answer: "No, for this is not what I am here to communicate to you. I am here to explain as best I can what the spirit world is like for Hans's and Philip's book, not to digress to other matters."

Question: "What about religion? Is there any and what does the spirit world think of our ideas about it, and what would seem to be the many bigotries in our world?"

Answer: "It is difficult for me to explain this to you in a way you will understand except to say this: There is no one real religion; there is only one real truth, and that is progression. All men and women are part of one God, and the Godhead is part of every man and woman. Progression ultimately leads to unification and wholeness."

Question: "I still do not understand what you are saying."

Answer: "Go away then, my dear friend, and think about it. What I have said to you is very simple. In meditation many in your world have come to understand what I have just said to you."

Question: "Do people in the spirit world class people on Earth as below and the spirit world as above as we do; and is it really positioned as we think of it, above our world?"

Answer: "The answer is yes and no. For in truth, yes, the spirit world is technically above you; and yet, examples of it are around you all the time. So many people in your world claim they have never seen a spirit person, but sometimes they materialize in such perfect form that if they walked past you in the street you would not even think there was anything unusual. From our side of existence this is possible, but as you look to your skies, think of the spirit world and know that many of us are there looking down upon you."

Question: "Why are people in our world not warned, from the spirit world, of the dangers or the awful things that can happen to them? Does the spirit world know of these things in advance, or don't they know either? Do the people who do sometimes get warned in our world get messages intuitively from spirits?"

Answer: "You do not pose one question but several. It seems many times I use this word to explain things to you—progression. Some things you must experience and have happen to you in your life, however painful or unpleasant they may be, in order to progress. Those who are needed in our realms to heal the sick would never have a feeling for the sick or crippled unless they had experienced these things in your life. Those who assist people who have been murdered or slain would never have the ability to assist in the same way unless they'd had such experiences themselves. It is true that you have loved ones on the second and third levels who keep close to your world and often keep an eye on their children and loved ones and who will contact mediums and even the individuals themselves, if this is possible, to try to warn them of difficult situations that are there for them. For some this is easier than others; for some, it is impossible, although in truth, those above them sometimes do not allow that communication to come through if it would affect the person's long-term progress to the higher levels of existence.

"Also remember those on the second and third levels also carry on their lives in much the same way you do. Of course, yes, we have intuitive spirits, mediums who have come over from your world who find it much easier to tune in with people from your level. In this world we love the mediums. Do you think we would waste such gifts just because the physical body is dead?"

Question: "Many people who come into the spirit world obviously have disabilities and illnesses. Would they be healed in hospitals, have operations and other treatments to make them well, or would they just think they are well and be on the way to normality?"

Answer: "This very much depends on how progressed you are when you come over. Obviously you would have to have an understanding of the higher levels of existence to be very quickly brought into balance. Let me say this to you: even if you had a leg or an arm or an eye missing in the physical world, if you were to understand progression and accept that there is life after death, then of course you would very quickly be brought to perfect balance. But however knowledgeable you are, it is often a fact that when you first come over to us, if you have been very ill, you do need rest and balance, and are received into the hospital sanctuaries that we have here. Operations as you speak of are carried out by surgeons who were in this profession in the body, and those who cannot readily accept advancement are drawn towards these people. Such physicians however are also great, keen minds who make wonderful advancements.

"I am impressed by your inquiry about being healed by the mind, and I tell you that, in truth, in all existences much healing can take place purely through the mind. I must say to you now that we have reached a stage where I cannot spend any more time answering your questions or strain further the abilities and gifts of your medium, Philip. Therefore, I wish for peace to be with you all. Goodbye."

CHAPTER 18

A COMMUNICATION BETWEEN A COUPLE REUNITED IN SPIRIT

This communication with Sam and Mabel was received June 10, 1998, at 1:30 P.M.:

Sam asked, "How long has it been since we were reunited, Mabel?"

Mabel was surprised by the question, but telepathically tuning to him realized he was trying to work it out as we would understand it by Earth time. Mabel explained, "Time is different here. We have no days, weeks, months, or years. We only recognize and accept time has passed when something important happens."

Sam, who was new to the spirit world, was still a little unsure about this. "Mabel, you know my love, one of the amazing things is that you look so very much younger. Indeed, you are as beautiful as the day I met you!"

Mabel found this very funny but enjoyed Sam's words. "I think you had better have a look at yourself. You've certainly changed from when you came over to us from the physical world."

Unfortunately, Sam did not seem to be able to remember and hadn't had a chance to look at himself in a mirror since he had come over. Strangely, Mabel did not seem to have any mirrors in her house. "Where are the mirrors?" he asked her.

"We don't have any," she replied. "We don't need them! The visions and our physical attraction for each other are just there for us, but we don't need to look in a mirror to see that. This is a big difference between the Earth world and ours, Sam. It's not what you look like, it's what you are that is important to us now, and we can be closer and blend more perfectly than we ever did in a physical way."

Mabel touched Sam's hand and he enjoyed this and felt sensuality and intimacy in a way he had not felt for a long while. He immediately progressed and learned a lesson about what blending meant.

"Mabel, I need that mirror," he said.

Having told him only moments before that such things did not exist, Mabel reached into a cupboard and produced the mirror. "There you are my dear. Look into it if you must."

He did and could not believe what he saw there. He was so much younger, perhaps twenty-two years of age again, his face and skin clear and bright, his eyes as sharp as they had been in his very best days. "I can't believe this!" he exclaimed. "How does it happen? What has happened? First I see you so young and beautiful, I wonder how I shall ever keep you, and then I look in this mirror and see that I am also changed in the same way."

It took Mabel a while to explain to Sam that they now lived in spirit and not in a physical dimension and that things were different. "In the physical world from the day you come into existence, decay and wastage happen, which is entirely the opposite side of the coin to the spirit world, for here every day you grow younger until you are back to your best years." However, she pointed out to him that this was not the case for all people. There were all different kinds of people who lived in this realm where they now existed, those who were happy and contented and those who were unhappy and discontent-ed, good people and not such good people. She also told him that he need not concern himself with this as like would always attract like and those who were not such good people would be together, and those who wished for kindness and protection would also be together in groups. Sam was very happy, particularly so at the prospect he was not going to get any older.

"Does this mean that you and I will just stay here together in this little house forever, Mabel?" he asked.

"Yes," she replied. "If that is all we ever want we could do that, but we must also have other things to do and other things to learn. There may come a time when we decide we would like to try to progress to higher levels or maybe to go back and experience the things that don't seem so attractive to us in the physical body. It may be that we choose to live other lives to make progress in that way. Also, Sam, often people go back to the physical world in groups. Maybe next time I will be your mother!"

Sam was adamant this was not what he wanted, and he wished to stay as he was now and with Mabel forever.

"We shall see," said Mabel. "We shall see."

One question that Sam very much wanted an answer to was this: if he was now in his twenties and in his optimal years, why was it he was seeing so many children, even tiny babies? "Do they stay like that?" he asked. "Or do they grow up into adulthood?"

Mabel explained that the moment a single sperm fertilized an egg in a woman's womb and physical life began, even if that life only lasted a moment and was lost to the spirit world, a new spirit being would come from it who would be cared for and live and be loved until that child came to its optimal years; then it would be sent back to live another life in a physical body.

All this seemed confusing to Sam as it probably does to us in our world, but at the same time, it made complete sense and had a marvelous truth to it. Sam had another problem. He had never believed in the spirit world but now that he knew it did exist, he wanted to show himself to his daughter so that she would know he was all right and had carried on; but how would she recognize him looking like he was twenty-two?

Mabel laughed and told him, "If you wish to appear as you looked when you came over then this is quite possible. Indeed, many people here choose to keep their elderly appearance, their grey hair and bent backs, because that is the way they feel happiest. By the same token, Sam, if you want a physique like Mike Tyson, then you can have it. The choice is yours!"

All of this was too much for Sam—indeed, he had much to learn! As time passed, he decided to study people and see if he could learn about the type of person they were by the way they presented themselves. Many times he would see people who appeared luminous, whose whole body would glow. These people seemed to have a look of perfect peace on their faces, yet they also appeared virile and confident. Sam hoped that one day he would be like this too. Quickly, with Mabel's help, he came to understand these were people who had made spiritual progress and attained great knowledge. Sam hoped with all his heart that one day he would be like this. Of course, this pleased Mabel for it showed he had a wish to progress.

Sam had always had an eye for women and Mabel had to smile when he said to her, "You know, Mabel, it's strange but none of the young girls here wear make-up or racy clothes, do they?"

Mabel smiled and replied, "Well, that's because almost everyone over here very quickly realizes natural beauty is far better than these things, and it is only in the very early days that those who have come over feel they need to use such things. What could be more beautiful than a young girl of seventeen naturally presented?"

"Mm! Yes, that is true!" Sam agreed. He had been surprised to see new arrivals who seemed uncultured and violent, perhaps what you could describe as of the primitive races, maybe such as those you would see in the Brazilian jungle. They arrived covered in mud and warpaint and were very aggressive, still carrying their spears and shields, appearing ready to kill whomever they saw.

Mabel explained that they would realize their friends were no longer like this and would greet them with friendship and smiles. Even these people from other tribes were very quickly changed and progressed, and perhaps it was with them that the changes could be taken note of, more so than anyone else.

Mabel and Sam are just an ordinary couple who have tried very hard to explain to us here on Earth, via Philip Solomon, the way life is in the spirit world, and I think we should be very grateful to them for giving us a wonderful insight into their life in spirit.

CHAPTER 19

A MESSAGE FROM RUDOLPH OVARAITH

This communication came on June 16, 1998, at 7:30 P.M., from Rudolph Ovaraith:

"Greetings, Philip. I am in the spirit world. My name is Rudolph Ovaraith. My last life was in Germany. I served in the German army and died on the Russian front outside Leningrad. It was a terrible time for the whole world and for humanity, but I will tell you this, Philip, the spirit world is wonderful. I am here with my wife, Helga, and follow the occupation of a professional musician, something all my physical life I wanted to do.

"In this world we have the opportunity to do anything we wish and to follow any occupation we feel suited to without the restrictions of the physical world. I travel and play with a professional orchestra, visiting our four 'cities' which are the place of mountains, the place of forests, the place of plains and fields, and the place of industry. I love to visit and give performances in each city. When I play my violin, I play it so well and sweetly, far better than I ever would have in my restricted time in the physical. Helga writes poetry and gives readings to groups, mainly in the city of mountains where we have chosen to live.

"Both of us drive small Volkswagon cars which we enjoy. We do not need them, but, oh, the pleasure of those little vehicles! We love them so much I think we shall never easily give them up! It is also my intention one day to work with the mediums of your world. That is why I am studying at one of the great halls of learning in the city of plains and fields under the tuition of a great teacher named Brogenberg, so that I may serve both spirit and Earth in the future. I am also working on a two-hundred-person project to bring about collective development of our higher spirituality so that I, with understanding, will eventually realize that I do not need things like my violin and my car. One day they will not seem so wonderful. It is very difficult. I love them both so much.

"Helga attends the 'University of Trees,' to gain—how shall I describe it to you—a degree so that she may have a better understanding and knowledge of holistic wisdom to help others. One day she hopes to be a recognized healer in this world and to pass her influence to those who follow the same practice in your world. This is possible for us, Philip, if we wish to link with the healers of your dimension.

"Do you understand me, that despite the things I am doing I still have so much to learn? The time when I was on Earth may seem a long time ago to you but here it is merely the twinkling of an eye. As an example, until recently I have always desired the company and the basic satisfaction of sexual intercourse with beautiful women. Even this is available to you here if it is something you wish for, Philip, and I tell you, in truth, I gorged my appetite until only very recently. I suddenly realized sex without love is meaningless and that Helga's love and affection were all I ever needed, and that lesson was learned. But I have so much else to learn; we all do in this spirit world.

"I also wanted to be one of the big bosses here, those who told others what to do, so they let me. I quickly learned that power without wisdom, experience, and compassion meant only stress and aggression, and it was only wanting that power that made me strive to be one of the big bosses, as I call them. I now know that only through experience, learning and compassion, and an understanding for others will I ever be a 'big boss,' like my teacher Brogenberg. He is so wise, you see, to see clearly what is right and wrong for people as individuals so that eventually they can offer the same wisdom to others. His boss must be very wise indeed and on a higher realm that is not known to me at this stage, though I wish it was, for he must be truly very great.

"I hope this information I have presented to you so openly, Philip, helps with the book that you and Hans are writing, and I hope my little outline of my experiences of spirit will be helpful to you both. *Auf Wiedersehen.*"

CHAPTER 20

CONVERSATION WITH
MARY OF MEDICI

This communication with Mary of Medici came on June 22, 1998, at 6:15 P.M.:

"Hello, Philip, my name is Mary of Medici. I understand you wish to ask me some questions?"

"Yes, I am grateful, Mary, and there are many things I would like to ask you. Can you tell me anything about the spirit realms that I have not already been told?"

"I can and I will," she answered.

"There is something that interests me very much. Who is in charge on your side? Is there a big boss, and is there a form of management that operates underneath that person, and, indeed, do they govern us in our world?"

"What a funny thing to ask me, Philip. We do not have bosses as such, but those you speak of are also the same ones that you would call angels from your understanding."

"Right, good. This is very interesting, Mary. So there are angels in the spirit world?"

"Of course!"

"What do they look like? I have seen what I think are angels and they seemed to have beautiful faces, beautiful wings, and send out the vibration of being perfect beings, surrounded by sweet spirit music."

"The vision you describe of angels is perfect, though I must tell you many of them do not have wings," she replied, chuckling. "This management, these bosses you speak of—yes, we do have a management structure in the way you speak of. Angels, or bosses, as high as the mighty archangels: the big boss being Michael, the management being Seraphim and Cherubim. These are your bosses and management."

"Mary, are you mocking me?" I asked tentatively.

"Of course I'm not, Philip, and if you feel that way then I am sorry. Let's start again. The Archangel Michael is the big boss, the highest of all angels. Also, know this, Philip, the name Michael means 'like unto God.' In your world there are many great books of wisdom. In the Old Testament, doesn't it tell you that it was Michael that God sent forth to lead Moses and the people of Israel away from Egypt and to their Promised Land?"

"Let me ask you then, Mary, is it not just Michael, but other angels who are part of this work?"

"Michael has legions of angels. Gabriel is also another great boss."

"Mary, I feel you are having me on, but these are questions that Hans has told me to ask you about—that ordinary people would like to understand who the bosses are."

"I do understand, Philip, and I am not mocking you. Gabriel is also an archangel and is a perfect angelic substance in every way. In the ancient Jewish language, Gabriel means 'the mighty hero,' and it was he who told the unsoiled Mary that she would become the mother of the Nazarene."

"By Nazarene, you mean Jesus, I take it?"

"Of course, and he is also a great boss, even higher than the angels. But let me continue with Gabriel. He also told the barren woman Elizabeth she would bring forth new life, and she did, the one known in your world as John the Baptist."

"Who are the Seraphim, Mary?"

"Seraphim are the Seraphim!" she answered, offering no further explanation.

"What is their role in the management then?"

"The Seraphim are mostly concerned with love and they are always glorifying and praising God."

"Can you describe what they look like?"

"That is impossible for me to do, for you would not understand the description, such beauty do they have. However, each has six wings, two to cover the face, two to cover the feet, and two to fly with, and they are so beautiful. You are no wiser for my description, are you, Philip?"

"Not really, but I appreciate the things you are telling me. Am I to understand then, that as bosses go, they are next in line to the angels?"

"Yes, that is so; in your management, as you call it!"

"Okay then, Mary, who is next in line after the Seraphim?"

"Ah, the next in your bosses' line would be the Cherubim."

"Can you describe them?"

"There is a description in one of your great books where a gifted one says that he looked and saw, over the heads of the Cherubim, something appear like a sapphire stone, and that the vision of a great throne appeared before him, and that he talked to the Wise One clothed in linen who said: 'Enter between the whirling wheels under the Cherubim and fill your hands with coals of fire.' In truth, Philip, the Cherubim have four faces: that of a cherub, that of a man, that of a lion, and that of an eagle; though usually they present themselves as visions of the cherubs, such as those shown in the many statues and pictures you have in your world."

"Is that all there is then of the angels?"

"No. There are many angels that look exactly as you do in your physical body, and these are also part of the management. These are the ones you call guardian angels, and they often talk and influence you to continually progress and move towards the Light and to do good things in your life. Not all in your world sense the positive and wise protection of their own individual guardian angel. Each and every one in your existence, and on the first two levels of existence, at some time have difficulties and narrow escapes that they are helped through by guardian angels. You do not always listen to your own inner voice, and lessons are to be learned from these experiences when you realize if you had, the difficulties that are now in your life could have been avoided or would not be so bad if you had listened.

"Especially in your world, Philip, there must be numerous people who have told you where they have avoided accidents and even death when something has stopped them or spoken to them a split second before the incident occurred. I know the book written by you and Hans has very little to do with religion, but once more I will quote the great book, the Book of Psalms 91:11: 'For He,' [the great boss, if you like], 'will give His angels,' [the management, if you like], 'charge concerning you to guard you in your ways. They will bear you up in their hands, lest you strike your foot against a stone.' This is the big boss, the boss and the manager of all, Philip, in the spirit world and in your world."

CHAPTER 21

MESSAGE FROM THEO

This communication came on June 25, 1998, at 3:15 P.M., with the spirit known as Theo:

"Good evening, Philip. I have made this communication to explain that your quest to know of the spirit world is good, but you should also know that there is a world in between your world and ours, a world I will call the in-between place. It is of this place I will give you much final information from us for your book.

"Many in your world have had what you call out-of-body experiences, often thinking they have died or passed to our existence from hospitals or places such as this. They never reach the spirit world; in truth, they reach this place I speak of, the in-between world. This world is in an area exactly between your world and my world and is surrounded by a brilliant white light. It is a place often experienced and described as being of perfect peace by those who come to this area but do not actually make the move into the spirit realm. In truth, it is part of the spirit world. I should make that clear to you.

"Do you not find that people tell you when they have the experience of almost coming to our world that they find it so beautiful that often they do not wish to return to their physical body? Yet the very moment that will is part of their consciousness, they find that they do want to return to their physical life. It is the one thing at the front of their mind—the wish to go home to their loved ones in the physical. I can tell you that there are times when people have a great struggle in coming back and finding themselves in their physical bodies, and returning to your world from the terrible experience of just having escaped death; and yet, very commonly, they no longer fear death for the rest of their lives knowing that there is something more that is beautiful.

"Of course, there are occasions in our world when we will order people to return back to their own world because they still have lessons to learn in the physical. Have not people described to you a feeling of great freedom, weightlessness, and peace—perhaps floating from their bodies on a wonderful silver stream that attaches the physical to the spiritual— and of being guided towards the most brilliant light, one you could not imagine until you see it? For in truth there is nothing in your world of such magnitude. Indeed, neither your Sun nor Moon are comparable.

"When you reach this world, Philip, you come to a gate. Once you have passed through this gate, you can never come back into the in-between area; you would pass from physical to spiritual, and, indeed, this is the boundary in the afterlife you enquire of. It is very attractive, for here gather on the one side of those gates all those you have loved and who have passed to the second and third level of existence; they are waiting to embrace you the minute you step through the gate and close it behind you. Some people who do not actually make this progression experience the situation of dreaming they open the gate and step into the other world and move down a long dark tunnel with a beautiful glowing light at the end of it. Though many in your world believe they have experienced the afterlife, they have not; for only when you spiritually pass through the gate will you step into the afterlife.

"When I made my progression many moons ago I had these same experiences stepping through the gate; my loved ones were there and joined me and took me forward towards a big beautiful light. There before my eyes stood my mother, my grandfather, and my great grandfather, all with someone who was obviously a Wise One. They all looked so vibrant, so young and happy, and the minute I experienced that unification and reunion . . . I have never felt so happy in all of my physical life. The garden we sat in just beyond this gate was so beautiful, adorned with flowers and plant life wonderful and indescribable to you in the physical sense.

"There are those in your world who come to this place, the in-between world, and talk of their near-death experiences. There is no such thing as a near-death experience, Philip. It is not their time, though many have the wish to join the spirit realms. Many will come straight up to the gate and peer through, and try to experience what is on the Other Side. There are those who will knock and call to be let in. Sometimes, from beyond the gate, loved ones will have gathered and help the living go back where they belong with a simple explanation that they cannot come through because it is not their time and that they must go back home to their loved ones in the physical. Often this is not remembered by the person.

"I will give you the experience of someone who was accepted through the gate and taken on to make progression to the spirit life. This will help you to understand. A few years back, Philip, one of your relatives was at work, sitting at his desk, and he had a massive heart attack. Everything suddenly went black and vacant. He told us he felt as though he was in a tunnel and was hurtling upwards towards a beautiful crystal clear light, though at the same time part of his consciousness saw fellow workers over him on the floor, beating his chest and trying to return his life to him. He heard someone scream for an ambulance and had the experience of someone beating on his chest again; then he had the experience of someone taking him to a hospital and trying to resuscitate him. He saw all the doctors and nurses around him. Suddenly he felt he had left the tunnel and he was in this place I have described as the gate.

"He came to the gate and felt it; it was beautifully textured wood, and it easily slipped open for him. Inside he saw many of your relatives who were waiting to accept him into the spirit world, together with many old friends he had not seen for many years, people he thought had died. Then in seconds he found himself in this wonderful garden with the trees and flowers I have told you about, and to the side, there was a small door that he knew he had to enter. He was met by a person here whom he knew to be his guide, a person exactly in human form, and yet he understood him to be of a higher wisdom, one who had always been there for him but only now was he actually seeing him.

"The guide told your relative to look neither back nor to the side but to confidently follow him through the doorway which led into another small area. At this stage, he felt that all the ones he had seen previously had joined with him, yet there were many hundreds of other people whom he felt were important to him but he didn't know who they were, smiling, clapping their hands, welcoming him, then parting, and allowing him to move forward to stand before someone he knew was very great. This was someone whom he could only hope that some day he would be part of; a spirit so great, that he could only be of the very highest order. 'Welcome!' said this being, and with that your relative became part of the higher spirit world.

"Philip, I hope this helps you because it is important for you to understand that there is this place called the in-between world. Many people think they have near-death experiences and they have gone to the spirit world, but they have not. They have gone to the place that I have told you about, but never come forward to that last little area I have just described; for if they do, they will truly be in the spirit world! I hope this helps you. This is the last communication we will grant you for now; but through this book, Philip and Hans, we will help bring this knowledge to your world. Know that spirit will always be with you. Goodbye!"

CHAPTER 22

CONVERSATION WITH LEE TRAVERS

My communication with Lee Travers took place on July 1, 1998:

"How are you, Philip? How goes it?"

"I'm very well, thank you. Who are you, my friend?"

"My name's Lee Travers, and I'm gonna tell you all about the things you want to know, even though there are some who'd tell me I shouldn't!"

"Okay then, Lee, that's very good. Thank you."

"Don't thank me, man, the pleasure's all mine. By the way, I'm on level one. It's a place you've heard quite a bit about, isn't it, my friend, Philip, buddy? Now I bet that scares you a bit, don't it?"

"No, not really Lee. I'm well protected and I don't fear the spirit world on any level."

"Oh good! It's nice to hear you're so confident. Perhaps you'd like a bit of hellfire and brimstone to come your way, or to meet a few of the demon-slinging characters who are forever dealing with damned souls—you know, chucking them into molten rock and what have you!"

"You know, I don't like being mocked or made a fool of, Lee. You see this as a chance to play games, don't you? But what I would suggest to you, my friend, is that you find another medium, because I'm not interested!"

"Hey, steady on, buddy, I'm only having a bit of fun with you! Let's start again shall we? My name is Lee Harvey Oswald."

"Is that really who you are, Lee?"

"No, not really. I'm playing again, aren't I? I'm Lee Travers."

"If you mess about again Lee, I am not going to accept your information."

"You will, Philip, because you want to know about this first level, and as I'm one of the people who is actually here in it, I'm one of the very few people who can actually tell you about it, aren't I?"

"Well, why don't you get on with it then? Just go ahead in your own words. What's it like?"

"Well, it's most excellent. You can find a lot of the things a man would like here; lots of depravity. Women, for instance, who would do anything a man would want. Anything, man! If I want to get drunk and fight, there's plenty of dudes more than happy to join me."

"So you basically live a life of debauchery and violence then?"

"Yeah, you've got it, ain't ya? And it's just great, ain't it?"

"Tell me, Lee, do you have a wife and children in your existence on this first level?"

"Nope! I had plenty of them things when I lived in your world—two wives and several children and lots of children with many other women who don't even know my name maybe!"

"Lee, you actually seem to be happy where you are. Is that so?"

"Course I'm happy. I've told you, everything a man could want is here for you. You just think of it and you get it!"

"Wouldn't you like to try and improve yourself and go onto a higher level at some time?"

"What for man? I ain't got no interest in all that spiritual crap! I'm more interested in coming back to your world."

"You mean to live another life and try to progress, Lee?"

"Of course not, man. What are you talking about? I want

to come back to your world to watch people and influence them to do things."

"Lee, you unnerve me in the way you put that. Do you mean evil things?"

"I don't think of it as evil, man. I think of it as pleasure. Yeah, sure, I like to do these things. If I can influence somebody to be violent, to punch and kick someone else, you know, I get a real physical kick out of it, even though I'm in a spiritual body."

"Are you saying to me you can feel the pleasure of that violence?"

"Yeah, course I do, man. And do you know what is one of my really favorite things?"

"No, Lee, tell me."

"I like to come back to your world and watch girls getting undressed, and girls and fellas making out. I tell you, man, I can almost feel it. It's one of the things that really makes me feel I want to come back to your place. That's more attractive to me than spiritual things."

"Let me get this straight then, Lee. You're saying you can come back and watch ordinary, everyday folk having sexual relations?"

"Yeah, course I can. Well, not always. It's much easier for me really to come back and watch the sort of people who are like me. Uninhibited, capable of expressing themselves sexually, and enjoying their bodies."

"Some of us would say that's a bit perverse, Lee."

"Yeah, man, that's because you're as inhibited and stupid as those people who mix up the word love with sex."

"But you also said you can watch girls getting undressed. Would that be anyone?"

"Sure, man, you've heard of ghosts, haven't you?"

"Of course. I have written a lot about these things, but that's not the same as a spirit. I know that."

"Sure it ain't, but you know spirits are there sometimes, don't you? Don't you think I can be in the girl's changing rooms or the swimming baths if I want to, and see the things I want to see that give me pleasure?"

127

"I think you are disgusting, Lee, and I don't like the things you are saying!"

"I don't care what you think, man!"

"Are all the people on that first level of existence similar to you then?"

"No, not all of them, just different from those suckers above us!"

"So you are aware there is another spirit world above you then?"

"Course I am, what do you think I am, stupid or somethin'? We've got folks here who've got real balls, man, the type of people who have murdered and who have the nerve to lead governments and countries into atrocities against thousands of people!"

"And you are telling me you admire that?"

"Yeah, course I admire that!"

"Tell me the sort of people you mean then, Lee. Give me some names of people I would know."

"Well, people like Hitler, he's pretty cool . . . and Julius Caesar."

"Julius Caesar? Come on, you're joking with me again aren't you? He wasn't an evil man."

"I never said he was evil, I just said he's spent time here, man."

"Well, let me ask you, Lee, what sort of things did you do when you lived in the physical world that got you this reward you're so happy about, living on this first level of existence?"

"I was just me, man. Yeah, I shot the president."

"You're joking with me again, Lee, you're being silly. You're pretending to be Oswald again, aren't you?"

"Who's to say Oswald shot the president, or a president! That guy was a real sucker! I tell you this much, mate: he ain't here!"

"So what did you do then?"

"When I lived in your world, you mean? I lived in a place called the Bronx, New York, where your buddy lives."

"Do you mean Professor Hans Holzer?"

"You can call him what you want."

"What was your job?"

"I had lots of jobs, man, mostly getting shut of people other people needed getting shut of!"

"What was your address in New York?"

"You don't need to know that, man. Anyway, I spent a lot of time living in a place called Chicago."

"What was your address there then?"

"You don't need to know that either. I've come to tell you what this first level of existence is about and I've told you haven't I? It's good, man! Lots of sex, lots of violence, and we still remain close to your world."

"How far away are you then, Lee?"

"Closer than you know my friend!"

"Who are the bosses on that first level? Who are in charge of you?"

"Nobody's in charge of us on this level. This ain't no prison, buddy. We just do what we want. When I was a kid in your world, the nuns and the fathers were always telling me about Heaven and Hell. I tell you, buddy, there ain't no Heaven and Hell; but if this is one place and the other levels are the other, you can give me this place every time!"

"If it is so good, why do you keep visiting the physical world then?"

"I tell you, buddy, there are plenty of people in your world who reach out to people like me for communication, and enjoy the sensation of linking with us as much as we enjoy linking with them. Course, what I would really like, Philip, is to work on a regular basis with a medium like you. Now, I could really get some things done if I had someone like you to work through!"

"That will never happen, Lee, though I am grateful to you for communicating and giving me a picture of what the first level of existence is. In truth, I don't think I would open my channel to you again, though I wish you well; and I would ask you to consider seeing things in a different way and to think of progressing. There must be those on a higher level who care about you and who would welcome your progress."

"Geez, buddy! Don't you get it? I've heard all these things

before—heard them in your world. I'm happy as I am. You're right, this is wasting time and I'm ending this communication; but I tell you this much, buddy, if you're gonna write this book, you oughta write it fair and square and give people the opportunity to know that there is a place for people like me to find happiness. Anyway, I'm outta here. See ya, sucker!"

CHAPTER 23

A VISIT WITH AL CAPONE

This communication with Al Capone took place on July 7, 1998, at 10:45 P.M.:

"Hi'ya, Phil, my name's Al Capone."

"Hello, Al. I wouldn't have thought you would have had an interest in spirituality and such things, Mr. Capone."

"Just call me Al. Never underestimate me, Phil. There's more to me than people thought!"

"Well, you were certainly a very well-known gangster, weren't you!"

"Nah! Never did that for more than about five years. You're on about Chicago and stuff, ain't ya? I had a bit of a go at things, perhaps about 1925 to 1931. About five years, that's all. And people said a lot of bad things about me that weren't true."

"You were a gangster though, weren't you? It's said that you killed people and committed a lot of crimes, you know?"

"Yeah, maybe so, but we only killed or robbed our own sort. I never killed anybody that didn't need killing! I was just a businessman in a dirty business."

"But you did bad things?"

"Sure, I did! That's why I came to the first level of existence."

"Right, Al, this is very interesting. Can you tell me about it?"

"You hold on a bit. I'll tell you when I'm good and ready!"

"Oh yes, sorry about that, Al; in your own time then. In all honesty though, don't think I'm being rude, but we don't really want people's life stories, even though I'm sure your life story was absolutely fascinating. It just doesn't mean too much for this book Hans and I are writing. We need to know about these other worlds and especially the first level of existence."

"Yeah, okay then, what would you like to know?"

"Well, for example, who took you over to the spirit world? Was it terrible going to that first level?"

"Yeah, I suppose it was, but it was perhaps where I deserved to come. Gotta learn things, haven't I?"

"Did you have people there that you care for, Al?"

"Yeah, plenty of gangster pals, I can tell ya! But it was my father that fetched me over. "

"What was his name, Al?"

"Gabriel. Now my old man, he really was an angel."

"So I take it he wasn't on the first level like you then, Al?"

"Maybe not. But anyway, he's the one that fetched me over. Nobody else probably could have got me to come over. I would probably have stayed close to your world. Always loved the booze, the dames, and the gambling, didn't I?"

"Are you not with your father or mother?"

"What are you talking about, boy? There's no way that someone like my mother would have come here. She's in the higher realms!"

"Who was your mother then, Al?"

"My mother was called Teresa, and she was an angel."

"Where did you all come from originally, Al?"

"Now you want me to tell ya Sicily, don't ya! But actually, I was born in Brooklyn. I'm a New York boy. I've got good friends like Paul Kelly and John Torrio here with me as well. What can you say? Where do you expect guys like us to go? We all loved the dames, the prostitutes, the gambling, and the drink . . . yeah, and the violence. And all those types of things are here for us on this level. Those are the sort of things that are important to us here. Mind you, I sometimes kinda wish I could be with May and Sonny."

"Who are May and Sonny?"

"May was my wife, a lovely Irish gal, and Sonny was my boy."

"So why the love of prostitutes, Al?"

"Ah! A guy called Big Jim caused all that stuff. Too many women made available to you and that, you know. Pretty faces that pox you up!"

"Well, that's one way to put it, Al!"

"That's the only way to put it, man. I tell you something, Philip, for somebody who ain't interested in my life and only wants to know about the spirit world you keep asking a lot of questions about it!"

"Do I? I didn't realize I was, Al, I'm sorry. Just one question then: Didn't they call you Scar Face because of that scar you've got? How did you get that? Was it in a fight or something?"

"That ain't something I wanna talk about and actually I got that in the First World War."

"Is that true, Al?"

"Look, I don't really want to talk about it."

"Okay, Al, are you still a gangland boss in the other world?"

"Course I am! I'm just as kind here as when I was in the body. Lots of people on this first level of existence you've been told about owe me plenty, and still I give them the things they want over here."

"Can you still drink and gamble and all that stuff then?"

"Yeah, course you can. You can do anything you want, and it's physical here, right there in front of you. You can touch it, feel it, and have it. We ain't that far from your world really, you know? That's why I don't join May and my boy in the higher levels. It wouldn't be right for me just yet. I need the physical things, and I need the edge of business. I'd like to come back to your world and feel and sense that as well. You can do that you know, if you want to."

"Yes, Al, so I've been told."

"Mind you, the guys in your world today ain't proper businessmen like we were! We went and sorted out our own problems. We didn't leave others to do our dirty work. If someone crossed me, I'd sort 'em with a baseball bat or send 'em to the fishes!"

"Fishes? What about fishes, Al?

"What's with you, buddy? We put 'em in the water, dead like!"

"Who runs stuff over there now, Al?"

"Who do you think, Phil? Who would you think? Me! Al Capone! I'm the Boss!"

"Yes, but apart from you?"

"Well, people from my time. You've had these things explained to you. The world goes on the way we would want it to."

"Can I ask for some names?"

"Er, people like Dion, Hymie, Bugs . . . come on boy, you've seen the films, you know these people as well as I do!"

"Yes, I suppose some of the names come to mind. But I always question my links to the spirit world and my imagination as well."

"Well it ain't, buddy. What you're hearing from me is real. We've got everybody here, and they all go on much the same as they did on Earth. You want to see my club here, Phil?"

"If that's an invitation, Al, it's very nice of you, but I think I'll give it miss; I don't fancy that first level of existence."

"Ah, that's bullshit! You listen to too many other people. We have all the fun here, and like I say, we're close to your world!"

"What about coming back here and living another life? Would you like to do that, Al?"

"No way, man. I can do anything I want here. Everything's easy and it's my kinda place. Understand, there ain't no jails neither! Ain't gonna be no Alcatraz here for me, boy!"

"Do you have a partner, Al?"

"If you mean a woman, I've got about seven coming round tonight, and I ain't decided which one I'll pick yet!"

"Are you having a joke with me, Al?"

"Nope, I ain't joking with you at all, buddy! I have everything here that I want; but it's like I say, the things you don't want you don't have to have either. Ain't got no tax. Ain't got no feds."

"You make it sound quite attractive, no doubt, to some people, Al, when everyone else has told me what a terrible place it is."

"Yeah, well, it's 'cos they'm all suckers, ain't they? They want to progress and learn and get to higher levels and be what they ain't never gonna be! Whatever I wanted in your world I took it, and whatever I want here I have it. This is my idea of Heaven and there are a lot of guys and gals who agree with me."

"What sort of home have you got, Al?"

"That seems a pretty dumb question to me. What do you mean?"

"Well, what I mean is, what sort of place do you live in?"

"I've explained this to you and told you whatever I want is here. I live in the sort of homes and hotels that I want to be in."

"Are they like bricks and mortar and wood?"

"Yeah, course, sure they are. Everything is just the same as it was in New York or Chicago."

"Is the time now or back in the twenties and thirties for you?"

"Yeah, twenties and thirties. I wouldn't want to live in your time although I come and have a look at it occasionally. The women ain't bad, but apart from that it's crap! You ain't got no idea how to have fun, you people!"

"Here's a question I would like to ask you, Al. If you are carrying on with your life as a gangster, a businessman, then you must still have police there; otherwise you wouldn't be able to act out your lives."

"We don't act out anything!"

"No. Sorry Al; what I mean is, carry on with your life the way it was."

"Yeah, yeah, course they're here: cops and jails. I just

don't like to talk about them! But we carry on and do things the way we want to anyway."

"All right. Another question I would like to ask you is this: is it possible for someone to be on two levels? How can I explain what I mean? Someone like Elliot Ness. Is he in your world or is he in a higher level?"

"He's in my world all right, the bastard! And I know what you're saying. Yes, I think it is possible he's on another level as well causing trouble!"

"What about travelling round, Al? Have you got a car?"

"Course I've got a car. I've got an armored car!"

"What does it look like?"

"What does it look like? What sort of question's that, buddy? It's a big black thing with gull wings and big head-lamps! What do you think it looks like? Weighs about seven or eight tons, armor-plated."

"Armor-plated? Well, you couldn't get shot in your world, could you? You couldn't get killed, could you, Al? So why armor-plated? "

"I've told you everything goes on exactly the same in this world as it did in your world."

"Well can you explain it to me a bit more clearly?"

"No I can't explain it any better! I've just told you how it is, haven't I?"

"Okay Al, sure. Are you studying things? Are you learning anything about spirituality and looking into progressing?"

"I'm looking into how to make money. I'm still in business and I'm happy as I am, as a businessman."

"You mean a gangster?"

"No, a businessman!"

"What about our world now, Al, is it of interest to you?"

"Sometimes, but life goes on here, so what the heck!"

"So listen to me, Al, are you telling me you are now more of a business man on the Other Side?"

"Sure, that's it, I'm running things real good now."

"And progressing as a person?"

"Yeah! And I'm trying to influence and help, but it's not

just me. Other people, I try to help them too, you know. Of course, they don't always listen. But the people in your world don't always listen, do they Philip! Tell them if they've got business down there, to keep things legit. That's the way, everything legitimate. Never take chances and keep things straight."

"But do you try to help people over here, Al?"

"I try to, the people in your world that I care about. And I tell you something as well. I'm a kind guy. I help lots of people, and I did when I was in your world as well. I looked after the old people of Chicago, don't worry about that, and plenty of the soup kitchens only had soup 'cos I give it 'em! And there were plenty of individuals in your world who'll tell you I was a regular kinda guy. Course, I still am, just misunderstood; especially when I had to do things that other people thought were bad. Well, business is business. But you tell me, Phil, what does it say on my gravestone, eh? What does it say on my gravestone?"

"I don't know Al, you tell me."

"It says, 'My Jesus, Mercy.' So I can't be a bad guy can I? But I'm where I want to be. I'm happy."

"Okay, Al. Well can I just ask you these last few questions then? Some people have described the first level of existence as being a terrible place, dark with no light, and full of evil people. How would you describe it?"

"Well, buddy, what can I say? You've just described Chicago, ain't ya? Or London, or Birmingham where you live? There can be parts of any city like that. I suppose it is like that to some extent, but it's where I'm quite happy to be, and I can tell you there are many people here who never want to go any higher and they don't wanna come back to your world either. They're quite happy where they are."

"Is there violence, and physical sex, and, how can I put this to you, you know, like gangsters who live what seem terrible lives to us ordinary, everyday people?"

"Yeah, course there are, but what can I say. That's what I'd call a great existence! I'm perfectly content with it, anyway. And that's about it, that's all I can really tell you about the spirit world on this level. I'm satisfied with it just as I was in my physical life. So I'll say ciao to you buddy."

"Okay, Al, thank you for that communication. Goodbye."

CHAPTER 24

INTERVIEW WITH JUDY GARLAND

This communication with Judy Garland came on July 9, 1998, at 7:30 P.M.:

"Hello, Philip, my name is Judy Garland."

"Well, Judy, it really is great to speak to you, I mean Miss Garland."

"No, just call me Judy, that'll do! They tell me you wanna know something of this world over here that we live in, what it's like, buster."

"Yes I do, Judy. It would be very nice if you could tell me what it's like in spirit."

"Well, it's just great, better than it ever was in the body!"

"So you prefer living in the spirit world than this one?"

"You'd better believe it, buddy! Course, I miss Liza and Lorna and I suppose everyone else that really loved me, especially the fans; but let's face it, Philip, I was gone at forty-seven and about five million dollars in debt, so they tell me. God knows where all the money went though!"

"You seem to be saying something there, Judy."

"Oh, I'm not saying anything; it's gone! It's passed! Let people say and think, in your world, what they will, I don't care."

"Who taught you to sing, Judy?"

"No one taught me to sing. I could always sing. My

grandfather could sing, my great grandfather could probably sing. No one taught me anything. I could just do, as far as the show business side of things were concerned. My problem was in doing life! Everyone expected so much. It was just stress all the time."

"So did you take your own life, Judy?"

"No, I was just so mixed up at the time; I wouldn't even have known how to have gone about it! Too many pills, barbiturates, whatever you want to call it. That's what it said on my death certificate, didn't it?"

"I don't know, Judy."

"And I wasn't alcoholic, either. I liked the old drink, but I could handle it too. I could always handle it. I'll tell you one thing more before I tell you a bit more about this world, Philip. The best show I was ever involved with was my own funeral because I came to that, you know!"

"Are you serious, Judy? Did you really go to your own funeral?"

"Course I did, and thank God for Frank Sinatra and Liza sorting things out! And I tell you this much, as long as you've got Liza, you've got me. In fact, at some time in the future I would like to think they will make a real film of my life, and Liza is the one I would like to play the part. But let me tell you more about this world."

"Thanks, Judy, it is what I really need. It is wonderful to hear your stories. So many other people have come through and always seem to tell me about this world and not enough about the spirit world. I would be really grateful if you could tell me what it's like."

"It's fantastic, Philip. Everything I ever wanted is here, but mostly love. Love is all I ever really wanted, to be loved and admired. I give performances here for thousands of people, bigger crowds than I ever appeared before in the physical world. And I don't need to swallow anything to make me happy, 'cos I'm happy all the time. Having said that, sometimes I like to be just a little bit sad. It's part of my personality you know; so if I want to, I feel a little bit sad! Ask me some questions, Philip."

"Thank you, Judy. Well, to start, can you still talk to your friends the same as you did in the body?"

"Yeah, course I can; but you just think about it and it's there, sort of telepathically, if you like."

"What sort of home do you live in? Can you describe it? Is it like bricks and mortar or wood?"

"No, not really. It's something like a fairy castle, that's the best way I can describe it. Something like you have in England, with lots of rooms where I can go and do and achieve anything I want. Practice my dancing, my singing, entertain my friends."

"How do you get around?"

"Well, I've always been a bit of a material girl in all honesty, and I like to be driven around. Cars always seem safer than anything else to me. In all honesty though, Philip, you've only got to think of somewhere and you can be there if you want to. But I do like a lot of material things and they are still there for me."

"Excuse me saying this, Judy, but you've been over quite a while now. But were you like this when you first came over, or did you feel sad, or was it what you expected it to be?"

"Oh, it was everything I expected it to be! But of course I've progressed, but I do still like a lot of material things, and I just think of them and they are there for me."

"And love, Judy? Are there people there that you are attracted to?"

"Goodness gracious me! Yes, of course! I've always been a great romantic. I'm sure that's in my spirit, Philip. I'm always falling in and out of love."

"Can you be with someone in a loving way?"

"Yes, of course, anything we could do in your world physically, we can do here, and falling in love is part of that."

"But don't you think that falling in love is part of a higher order as well?"

"Yes, I do, and in this world it is perhaps a more real love."

"Judy, are there motorways and highways and that sort of thing there?"

"Philip, you must try to understand, and I can't tell you any different from what anyone else has told you: whatever you want is there. If you want to be going up the highway in a cab, then it's there for you; but if you want to just think of being on top of a beautiful mountain, singing and dancing, then you can do that, too, and it's there for you instantly. Such is the spirit world."

"Does it feel physical, Judy?"

"It feels however you want it to be."

"This is a bit difficult for me, Judy, but you know my friend, Hans Holzer . . ."

"Well, I know of him through this book you guys are writing, of course."

"Well, he always asks me to ask whoever comes through, famous or otherwise, to tell me what the spirit world is like, because we assume it is different to our world, of course."

"Well it is, Philip, inasmuch that it is the spirit world, but it is almost a mirror, really, of your world. The only difference, as I've already said, is that whatever you want is there for you. Let me think of a word to describe it. Mm, yes. In the physical world people often speak of paradise where anything good that you could possibly imagine would be there for you. That's the way I would think of it when I was a little girl. Well, in the spirit world that's exactly how it is, and everything that is down below is up above too if we want it. Course, there are other orders, other higher levels of the spiritual realm where people are just like pure energy. But I am a performer, so I think I will be staying here a little longer!"

"Well, thank you for coming through, Judy. It's been lovely speaking to you."

"Just before you go, Phil, would you like to have a quick word with Frank Sinatra? We're actually working on a show together."

"Yes, of course I would. Hello Frank."

"Hello, Philip. I hear you've had a word with Al Capone."

"Oh, you know about that then, Frank!"

"Well, you be careful, my boy. They'll treat you like they did me and they'll think you're one of the Mob. Don't worry, fella, I'm only joking with you! Good luck with the book. Ain't Judy just great?"

"She is, Frank."

"You know, I told them when she passed over from your world she'd have a mystic survival. She was absolutely number one, the tops. When they forget the rest of us they'll never forget Judy, and you ain't, have you?"

"That's very true Frank."

"Anyway, bye for now, Philip."

"Bye, Philip." Judy's voice came in.

"Goodbye to you both and thanks for coming through."

CHAPTER 25

A TALK WITH BERYL REID

This communication with Beryl Reid came on July 18, 1998, at 7:45 P.M.:

"Hello, Philip, Beryl Reid here."

"Hello, Beryl. How are you?"

"Very well and you?"

"Quite good really, but I'm having a job to get this book together, you know!"

"Hm! It's a bit different, isn't it?"

"You know, I wouldn't have expected you to come through about something like this, Beryl."

"Why's that?"

"Well, you know . . . I just wouldn't have expected you to."

"Oh, I've always had a bit of an interest in the old spiritualism, you know, Philip! How's Birmingham doing?"

"Quite well really."

"What about Rustie Lee and Toyah; what are they up to?"

"I don't really know Toyah that well, Beryl, but Rustie's doing okay. She's just finished doing South Pacific and Bloody Mary."

"Yes, yes, so I believe. Give her my regards."

"I will, Beryl. And what about you? What are you doing in the spirit world?"

"All the things I was too busy to do or couldn't do in my life, Philip!"

"Such as?"

"Lots of far more serious parts, and I'm writing a book like you."

"Really, Beryl? What's it about?"

"Well, I've just said about being serious, but this is comedy really. It's about a young girl who was brought up in Manchester and then goes to live in Scotland, right up in the wilds!"

"It sounds as though it will be very interesting. Beryl, didn't you come from Birmingham?"

"No, like my book says, I was born in Manchester, but I always loved Birmingham, especially the Hippodrome."

"Oh, yes, of course, I know that theater well."

"The thing is, of course, it's much easier for me to write my book here, Philip, than it ever would have been in the body, though I did write one or two books and I wrote a lot of material. I was actually bloomin' dyslexic, but when I was a kid they never knew about these things you know! You're not a very good speller are you, Philip?"

"How did you know about that, Beryl?"

"Ah, you'd be surprised, I know about lots of things! But you've just got to get on with life, haven't you?"

"Yes, I suppose so."

"Here, I just think of the words and the book unfolds itself. A lot easier than writing down there, I can tell you!"

"I certainly like the sound of that, Beryl. You know, I always thought you came from Birmingham."

"That was because I used to play a character called Marlene, but you don't remember that, do you? It would have been before your time."

"Actually I do, Beryl. My mom was a big fan of yours."

"Your mom was a great medium as well, wasn't she, Phil?"

"Yes, that's right. My mother, Elsie; I don't think there was ever a better medium, not that I've ever known anyway. Well, come on Beryl, tell me a bit about what the spirit world is like and what you do up there. Have you got some theaters?"

"Oh, we've got some great theaters, Philip, and often we

perform in theaters that are more like the Roman amphitheaters, great big wonderful outdoor places. At the moment I'm actually working on a film as well as the book. A bit of a follow-on to *The Killing of Sister George*. Do you remember that one?"

"I do, indeed, it was a great film. You played the part of an actress who was a lesbian, playing the part of a nurse, didn't you?"

"Yes, that's the one. Only this time the nurse is more like Marlene, the Birmingham woman."

"You're joking!"

"Yes, of course I am. Really, it is quite a serious film that I'm working on, but I haven't got it all sorted out yet."

"Are there great cities up there in the spirit world, like we have down here, Beryl?"

"Well, Philip, anything you want is up here really."

"You say that you were brought up in Manchester. Is there somewhere that looks like Manchester, England?"

"Yes, we have cities like that. All different cities, some like your own in Birmingham, or like London, or New York. What you want is what you see. Actually, in the body, my parents were Scots; father from Aberdeen and mummy from Edinburgh. If I was to think of those places and associate them with my parents, those are the sort of places I would see."

"But would they be real? Would they really be there, Beryl, so that you could reach out and touch them?"

"Oh yes, of course, everything would be exactly as I thought of it."

"So the spirit world is solid then?"

"These are the same questions you have asked everyone else, aren't they?"

"Yes, but Hans has asked me to do this."

"But can't you and Hans take it on board, that in the spirit world it is almost exactly the same as in your world. Whatever we want is here. Would you want me to tell you it is different to what it really is? I cannot tell you lies, can I?"

"No, of course not."

"You understand that I am speaking to you from the second level of what you perceive to be the spirit world?"

"Yes, I think so, Beryl."

"Is it things of a higher order that you wish to know of, higher levels? For if it is, I must tell you in truth, my boy, that no medium will ever be able to explain it to the people in your world. Communication between your world and the higher levels is not really possible; only tiny little snippets of wisdom are ever received, and only by those of the very highest order of mediumship."

"Could I do that, Beryl?"

"You are a wonderful medium between our world and your world, Philip, but even you would only get snippets from the higher levels."

"I find that quite interesting, Beryl, for it answers something for me that has always been a bit concerning, you know, around my own mom."

"What's that, Philip?"

"I'm always disappointed that I don't get direct contact and am not able to have a conversation with her the way I do with other people from your world. She always told me that she knew she would progress to higher levels when she passed over, so I assume that she must have done so, so I cannot communicate with her as I would wish."

"Well, yes, of course, that's what I'm saying to you, isn't it? And it explains how things are. All I can tell you is it is really beautiful here and we are all surrounded by love, and that we are all given the opportunity to progress to higher levels, and that if we choose we can come back to your earthly life again, to learn the things we didn't learn the first time round, if you like. But the gifts and things we were special at, including myself I hope, as an actress and comedienne, we do not lose these wonderful gifts. They are things that have been given to us by the Godhead and they continue and go on. Like me, just trying to continue and do the things I am best at, learning and progressing at the same time. Anyway, I've got to go now, Philip, so good luck with the book. Don't forget to get your spelling mistakes double-checked, and dot all the i's and cross all the t's. All the very best to you and Hans."

"Thanks very much to you, Beryl. Goodbye."

CHAPTER 26

CONVERSATION WITH JOANNA

This communication with Joanna happened on July 19, 1998, at 6:45 P.M.:

"Hello, Philip."

"Hello, Joanna. Who are you?"

"I am a spirit who will help you and your friend."

"May I ask you some questions, Joanna?"

"No, Philip, I only come to speak."

"Okay then, go ahead."

"Philip, may I ask you, sometimes do you open your eyes while you are linking with us on the Other Side of existence and do not two pictures seem to be there in your mind's eye?"

"Yes, I have experienced that."

"Let me explain then what has happened to you, Philip. Our world is at times very close and vibrates right next to your physical world, so it is no wonder that two visions are possible. I must also tell you that most of the time the inhabitants of all different existences are totally unaware of anything or anyone else being there whatsoever; only mediums, like yourself, occasionally see glimpses of both worlds."

"You are saying to me then, Joanna, that there are those in the spirit world who are equally unaware of us in the physical world."

"Yes, Philip, that is so. There are learned ones above and

learned one below. There are those with knowledge amongst your scientists who know physical matter is no more than vibrating atoms which, when appropriately perceived, can be seen as solid. The gap between the physical and spiritual worlds can be no less complex or simple, depending upon your understanding and ability to perceive, and as a medium you will understand that the vibration of spirit people is much greater than physical people, yes? Do you not know that, and understand what I am saying to you, Philip?"

"Yes, I do understand what you are saying, Joanna. When I work as a medium, I have to quicken my vibration so that I can attune and communicate with your side of existence."

"Is it not also true, Philip, that many of your readers will think that body and mind are purely physical? Of course they are not; it is spirit based from the very start of existence and only temporarily in an overcoat of physical bondage."

"This is interesting, Joanna, but tell me of your life in the spirit world. Who are you? What do you do?"

"I am a woman in my middle years. Twenty-five to twenty-eight is the way you would perceive me if you could see me, which you can't, can you?"

"No, that's true Joanna, I can't see you, I can only hear you."

"I came to the spirit world as only a little girl, about ninety years ago."

"Yet you say you appear to be about twenty-eight, Joanna?"

"Others will have explained to you that we move towards an optimal age, which is our middle years, but in truth I am now reaching a stage where it may be I will come back to your world to live another existence with a group of people I have spent time with in this world."

"Is that common, Joanna? Do you often come back in groups?"

"Yes, this is quite a common thing that happens, though not always in the same way that we have lived before. A father could easily become a mother, a daughter could become a son, a son could become a father, an uncle could become a niece. Many experiences must happen to bring people together, but there are people on progressive states who are meant to be brought together. Have you not had the experience, throughout your life, of people from when you were a little child coming into your life and spending time with you and being of importance to you?"

"Yes, that is true, Joanna."

"And throughout your progression in your physical life, has not someone come into your life to help just at the right time?"

"That is also true."

"This, Philip, is part of the great progressive state of reincarnation, and I am afraid that is all I really have to communicate to you at this stage."

"Thank you very much, Joanna, I am very grateful for it. Goodbye."

"Goodbye, Philip."

CHAPTER 27

MESSAGE FROM FRANZ

This communication with Franz came on July 29, 1998, at 9:30 A.M.:

"Who are you, spirit friend?"

"My name is Franz. I am a spirit who is willing to speak to you, to communicate with you, and one who has done much with the mediums of your world."

"How old are you my friend?"

"I am ancient, yet I am young. Your understanding of time is different from ours."

"Have you lived in our world, Franz?"

"I have lived many times in your world, as you have lived many times in your world, Philip."

"Can you tell me in very simple terms so that I can understand, what the world you live in is like now, Franz?"

"That is not easy to do, for there is nothing in your world that I could present as an example."

"Ah, this is very interesting to me then, Franz. So I take it you are not on the first, second, third, or fourth levels of existence. You come from somewhere higher?"

"You are wise and astute, Philip. But you do not need to be cunning with me, for I will tell you plainly and simply of my existence. It is true I do come from a higher level of existence than these places; and my world is of an order of higher consciousness, and I am also greatly privileged to be part of the great teachers who often help and guide you in your world."

"So you are saying to me, Franz, that spirit people are close by us and guide us. Is this a daily thing or an occasional thing or only when we need it?"

"Be assured and confident, Philip, in telling the readers of your book, that we are always there influencing you. How could we do anything else? Have you not been told that you are part of oneness, that you are part of us and we are part of you? Our help and advice come to you through the power of individual direct thought, although sometimes we have to work through mediums such as yourself to try and help people progress and see things more clearly. That is why mediums are so important to us."

"Are you what we call a guide then, Franz?"

"The term is good that you use."

"It seems from other mediums, though not in my experience, that most of these guides they speak of are Red Indians, religious leaders, ancient Egyptians, and people of this nature. Is this so?"

"Why do you ask me questions that you know the answer to, Philip? The answer, of course, is that they are not. Much that is passed on and spoken of through unreliable mediums comes from their own imagination, or, even worse, is given to impress other people in their existence. Remember that not every medium can work as well as the great ones and that they are on different levels of development."

"So the majority of mediums in our world are false then, Franz?"

"Philip, you must tell the readers of your book they should exert great caution. This is not something I would spend time working with you on for I have sent the same influence and knowledge through to your great friend, Hans Holzer, who even before he was reunited with you again in this life, has written many books advising people of what is good, what is wrong, and what are real mediums."

"I accept that, but I need to question you further, Franz.

So are you saying that these guides are purely imaginary visions in the minds of these so-called mediums?"

"Yes, exactly. That is a clear description. In their mind, if they think of an ancient Red Indian, then that picture may well be there for them; yet this vision has no real personality or existence, so that sometimes the imagination gets in the way of real psychic ability."

"I know this a difficult question that I am going to have to ask you Franz, but who is your boss?"

"Do not be embarrassed to ask such questions. In truth, I know the questions even before you ask them, Philip."

"Thank you, Franz. These are the sorts of things that Hans wants for the book."

"Of course. I am influenced by the presence of the Great One who is perfect above all."

"It still doesn't really tell me who you are talking about though, does it? Is that God?"

"Yes, my son, call him or her God, if you wish."

"Okay then, so who are the under bosses, Franz?"

"There are many with great wisdom, my friend, who influence and govern all worlds, yours and mine. But there are no presidents or prime ministers here or governments as you would understand them. For us it is pure love that drives us, and a combination of souls merging and working together to ultimately move towards oneness."

"Okay then, Franz, how do you have influence over my world?"

"Quite simply, I wish myself to be upon the vibration of your Earth plane, which is slow and uncomfortable at times for me, and I attach to the vibration of someone who is known in your world as a medium—someone like yourself. Then a very gentle merging of mental and spiritual attunement takes place and I am allowed to inspire mediums such as yourself with my thoughts and words. But be assured, Philip, it is all only ever achieved with the willing cooperation on the medium's behalf."

"I think I am so lucky that I can see, sense, and hear the spirit world, Franz, but how can others receive this gift?"

"What you ask, Philip, is difficult, for it is a gift that is very hard to receive. Relaxation and meditation must be practised to achieve such states, but also you must have great love and care for your fellow men and women, and the true medium must wish to help all, even those he or she would not describe as nice or worthy. Do you understand me, Philip?"

"Yes, I think I do, Franz."

"Perhaps the most important thing you could tell the readers of this book is this: remember, their loved ones and even those on a much higher level of spiritual progression are only a thought away and will always guide and help if asked. Also, never forget the power of prayer. Have we ever failed to answer you in your hour of need, or provide those who could help you to go forward in the things you wished to do that were for the good?"

"No, that is true, Franz. I have always received help."

"Goodbye then, Philip, until we speak again."

"Goodbye, Franz, and thank you for the information you have given me."

CHAPTER 28

MESSAGE FROM JOHNNY

Johnny's communication came on August 1, 1998, at 10:45 A.M.:

The spirit who called himself, simply and plainly, Johnny, communicated on August 1, 1998, with a simple wish to tell of his life on Earth and in spirit. In the body, Johnny had lived the life of an earl. Rich, respected, and honored, he was a man who would even see one of his daughters marry a man destined to be the king of his country. Johnny had been married twice, both times to beautiful society women of aristocratic breeding and bearing, yet despite all this seemingly wonderful existence, he had never been a happy man.

Everything had seemed too easy, served on a silver spoon, if you like, for most of his life. Then suddenly, without warning, his middle-age was blighted by ill health. In his words, "what was the point of it all?" This he had asked himself many times, especially in the last two or three years of his life when he had been able to do little of the things he had enjoyed as a younger man. But apparently Johnny was to find the answer to "the point of it all" and he wished to pass this on to us from the spirit world. Hopefully, we would see what "the point of it all" was, too. This is the story he told me:

"When I arrived on the Other Side, I was angry. I did not wish to come and leave my new wife over on your side.

"'How dare you fetch me?' I said to what seemed an old man I vaguely remembered as a servant. 'How dare you fetch me?'

"'It's no good, sir, you've got to come,' the old man replied. 'Don't you remember me? I'm John, the old footman? I served your family for over forty years.'

"'No, I don't!' I snapped. 'Take me to someone in authority immediately!'

"'Very good, sir, very good,' said old John, and led me in to what seemed a shiny room filled with many of my former relatives, including those I had long since thought dead. My father, my grandfather and grandmama, and my dearest mama were all there.

"'How good it is to see you, Johnny,' they all said.

"'How good it is to see all of you,' I replied. 'But tell me, does this mean I am dead?'

"My relatives nodded. 'Yes, it is basically as you say. But not dead; you are simply reunited with us in spirit.'

"I turned to my father and said, 'Daddy, this will be difficult you know, who will decide who is lord now? Surely it must be me as I have been lord for nearly fifty years. But that would be difficult with you here as well, wouldn't it, father? And grandfather . . . surely he will have something to say about that?'

"My father smiled and replied, 'I am afraid, Johnny, that none of us are lords here. We are just simple, ordinary everyday men and women. The life that you lived was just a wonderful example for you of learning.'

"'Of learning?' I exclaimed.

"'Yes, learning. You may find it is your destiny in the future, Johnny, to go back and be very, very poor, in the world you call Earth.'

"'Poor? Like a peasant, do you mean?' I asked with some disdain.

"'Indeed. For how could anyone, except a peasant, fully appreciate and understand the life of a lord, and how could a lord really feel sorry for a peasant, unless he had lived such a life himself? It is very early days in your progression and these

156

things are difficult for you to understand now, Johnny, but you will,' my father assured me.

"And I must tell you, Philip, that I did, and very quickly I came to understand what my father had said to me; and although I have been passed over for only about four or five years, I think those who have helped me over here would say I have progressed quickly. But in my life I did not show enough kindness to others in real ways. Although I always tried to help those in need when they were brought to my attention I did not go out of my way to help those in need, if you understand what I am saying, Philip."

"Yes, of course I do, Johnny, and I am sure you did help people."

"Thank you, but you see, not like my daughter. Now she was a real wise one, only lent to your world, I'm afraid."

"What was her name?"

"That's not really important in this communication. This is more to help you see the point of things and how things can have meaning for us when we come here and also when we come back to your world."

"Okay then, Johnny, tell me about your life in spirit. What do you do now? Are you still an earl or lord? Do you have servants? What sort of life is there for you, and what are your plans for your future?"

"Yes, wise questions as always, Philip. You show much initiative and understanding of us on this side and my plans for the future are what you might call reincarnation."

"So you intend to come back to our world?"

"Oh yes, yes, of course. But the next time I come back it will be as a very poor man."

"Will you remember you once lived as a lord when you come back to us?"

"No. I am told I will not have perfect understanding and remembrance of what I did before, although we do get glimpses, little feelings of past lives, of course. This is what people experience when they speak of having felt past lives."

"I see, that is very interesting. And you don't wish to stay in the spirit world, or to carry on where you are? I've been told that no one wishes to come back from the spirit world once they have died."

"That is a different thing. Of course the spirit world is so wonderful that no one wishes to come back immediately, but if you wish to progress and learn, then your world is the place where a lot of that learning is done."

"So, Johnny, what do you do in your everyday life now?"

"Well, I am reading lots of books and learning the art of communicating with the mediums in your world. Very interesting that is, you know. Made friends with a very famous scientist and writer, a man called Oliver Lodge. A great friend of my grandfather, don't you know—or was that my great-grandfather? Oh, I don't know! What does it matter? I've also got my old MG sports car over here. Love her, the old girl, you know, Philip; and how I love to spend time with my daughter. So much fun. Never a quiet moment with her. Wonderful!"

"So it's not sort of . . . well . . . all spirituality and serenity then, Johnny, you know, the way a lot of people have described the spirit world?"

"Oh no, it's not like that for me, Philip, not at all! And I would have no wish for it to be like that either, goodness gracious me, no! Always liked a bit of fun in the body, don't you know, and I'll tell you, Philip, I'm still up for the game while I'm over here! Though speaking of spirituality and serenity, I am reading books about those subjects, but a life without fun and frolics, I don't think so! But you see, Philip, things are whatever you wish them to be here. You just think about what you want and it's there for you, old boy. Our world is whatever you would want it to be."

"Tell me more about reincarnation then, Johnny, and what you've learned."

"Well, basically, those who come here to the spirit world have often lived many lives in your world. It's a chance to see lots of other sides of life, isn't it really? I'm coming back, next time, so I will basically understand what it is like to live . . . well, what can you say . . . in other ways. Look, here is an example for you, old boy. My cousin George was always a bit of a bounder, you know, always saw girls as good for one thing, so I said to him, 'George, why not go back as a girlie? It would do you good, old man, to learn to respect them!' Do you see what I mean Philip?"

"Are you serious, Johnny, is that the sort of conversation you had with your cousin?"

"Oh yes, certainly! Absolutely, Philip! It will help him to learn. Surely you can see that?"

"Yes, of course I can, Johnny."

"It's like another one of my family, a bit of a racist, if you know what I mean. Always thought that people who were a bit dark were of less quality than himself. Now you see a wonderful way for him to learn would be for him to come back and be black or something similar. He would quickly learn what an awful thing it is to hate someone just because they are different from you or because of the color of their skin. You would damn quickly learn, wouldn't you, Philip, if you had such remarks and downright racial hatred to contend with?"

"Yes, of course, I see that, and it is a wonderful thing you are suggesting he might have the opportunity to do that."

"Yes, the same way that someone has a disability or comes back and suffers in that way in another life. What better way to have care and feeling and understanding for the afflicted than to feel it for yourself in an earthly experience? And remember, Philip, time is not the same here for us as it is for you. We have time to think about these things. Time is short in your world and these are quickly learned lessons over here. Hm! You know, it is making me think, even speaking to you through your mediumistic channel. Yes, maybe I'll come back like my old Uncle Henry. He was crippled from the war, you know, and always had to walk with a stick. Could never really bend his knee, and we children never did understand him in the way we should have. He could be ever so grumpy, but perhaps he had good reason to be. Hm! Perhaps I will come back as a cripple, and quite poor. I would have to think about being black. I'm not quite sure about that at this stage of my progression! Anyway, got to rush, old boy, so I'll say toodle-oo and wish you all the very best of British luck with the book. Bye!"

"Thank you, Johnny. That was very enlightening. Goodbye."

CHAPTER 29

INTERVIEW WITH JENNY

Jenny's communication came through on August 7, 1998, at 9:15 A.M.:

Jenny, a little girl who passed over to the spirit world, told me her story and presented some wonderful words of wisdom in the way only, perhaps, a child could.

"Hello, Philip," she said in what was obviously the voice of a small child.

"Hello," I replied. "What's your name?"

"My name is Jenny. Will you tell my mommy and daddy that I'm okay and that I love them very much?"

"I'm sure they already know that, Jenny."

"They don't, you know, Philip. They think I'm finished, that I don't exist anymore, but I want them to know I do. It is very important to me that they should know I'm all right. But just tell them. Don't put their names in your book. Will you promise me that you won't?"

"Okay then, Jenny, I will find a way to tell mommy and daddy what you ask. I promise you I will do that and, as you ask, I will not name them in the book."

"Good! And can I tell you about my life here?"

"Yes, indeed, Jenny. Nothing would please me more. Just go ahead in your own words."

"Well, these days I spend lots of my time with my nanna,

she's my mom's mom, and I really do love my nanna, but I still have to go to school you know!"

"Do you? Well, that's very interesting. Tell me, how old are you?"

"Hm, I was nine when I came here and I've not been here that long, perhaps nine and a half or ten. I also play my piano and my guitar every day, and play with our old dog Benjamin. But I so often think of my mom and dad and little brother, and even though I am very happy here, it makes me sad because when I think of them I can see my old world and all my family who live there but they never see me or answer me at all. My nanna says I am gifted and if I had lived longer on Earth, I would have been a great medium."

"Do you understand the concept of a medium?"

"Yes, of course. My nanna was a medium and teaches me about such things."

"Speaking of teachers, do you have teachers for lessons like when you lived here?"

"I have many teachers here, but not at all like at my old school. These ladies are more like aunties than teachers, and they get you to learn and do the things that are good for you without having to be shouted at or grumbling. I really do love my teachers here!"

"That's lovely, Jenny. What sort of things do they teach you then?"

"Lots of things."

"Do you mean like reading, writing, and arithmetic; do you still learn those things?"

"Yes, I do, but we also learn many things we wouldn't have in your world, even things that can be difficult, like why I had to leave my mommy and daddy and come to this world and why some people don't seem to be so fortunate as others in my old world. All the time you are learning new things. All the time you are also learning why you are in existence and why you are a person, even though we are only little."

"So you sort of learn the point of being you, Jenny. What you are going to do with your life?"

"Yes. When I grow up I am going to be either a facilitator or a teacher."

"What's a facilitator, please, Jenny?"

"Oh, Philip, you are funny. Don't you even know that! It's someone who can talk to people like you for people over here. But not just like I'm doing today, it's for everyday. That's a facilitator, silly!"

"Oh, I'm very sorry, young lady. But truly I did not know what you meant. Let me ask you about the other things you speak of then. What sort of things would you do if you became a teacher?"

"I don't know, teach the way the aunties teach I would think, perhaps. But I would also like to be involved in the care of the animals in our kingdom, helping creatures like Ben find a home and happiness."

"That's interesting. Tell me, Jenny, do all animals come to your place, your world?"

"Not all. Perhaps all pets would, but wild animals go to another reception place, and lovely animals like our Ben who loved us in our earthly world will always be with us."

"Jenny, I once had a dog called Tina. Is she in your world?"

"Well she's not with me. But did she love you?"

"Yes, of course she did. She also loved my children."

"Then of course she's here, silly! But probably with your nanna or someone like that. "

"Okay, Jenny, here's another question. Do you have lots of friends around you?"

"Yes, lots of them, and we spend lots of time playing together and then studying together before relaxing with our families like I do with my nanna and grandad; and that's the way I shall stay until I grow older and wiser and then I shall come back to your world or go up."

"What do you mean, Jenny? Come back and live in this world? Is that what you are saying?"

"Yes, of course, and live with a new mommy and daddy. Sometimes you can come back and be a baby with your own mom and dad again, but you have to be very special to do that, with special work to do in the Earth world, because just for you it might not help you to learn something new to live the same life over again."

"Yes, okay, Jenny, that makes sense. Do adults come to your classes?"

"Oh no, of course not. Adults do not come to our classes."

"Why not?"

"Because we are very special. When we came here we were very young, some of us were only like little babies, others of us not more than twelve or thirteen years old. As children we can meet the wise ones from Heaven."

"How do you do that?"

"They visit us at school and we have special meetings with them to see if we can straightaway, or very soon, join them in Heaven; that's going up, but only children like us can do that. Well, except for some very special and kind ladies and men from your world."

"Do you mean like saints?"

"I don't know what you mean, Philip."

"Never mind, Jenny, it's not important. So you are sad at times and miss your parents?"

"I do, but it upsets me even more that they get upset, especially Dad, when they take the flowers to my grave. So many times I have stood beside him and shouted, 'Dad! I'm not there. Don't waste your money on flowers.' I was so lucky to be my dad's girl. If I can, I will be my dad's girl again. But even if I have become special and go up to Heaven, I will always help my daddy in any way I can, and Mommy as well of course. Philip, I can't talk any more for now. It's time for me to go to school."

"Okay, Jenny. Thank you for a lovely message and the information you have taken the time to give to me, I'm sure it will be a lovely message for all moms and dads who have lost a child to know they always go on. Goodbye and bless you."

CHAPTER 30

MESSAGE FROM THE SPIRIT PAUL

This communication with the spirit Paul took place on August 15, 1998, at 7:30 P.M.:

"Hello, Philip. Greetings. My name is Paul."

"Hello, Paul."

"Philip, ask me now the questions that are to the fore of your mind."

"Okay, Paul, I will do just that. Can you tell me who is the boss in your world? Who is the leader, if you like?"

"The same one that is the boss of your world."

"Okay then, Paul, who is he?"

"He is everything and everyone, but in your world the concept would be well placed and exampled by the one you called Jesus, the perfect essence."

"You know, somehow, Paul, I knew you would say that to me; but one problem for me and others is that everything we know about Jesus was generally written by other people many years after his life. I have always thought to myself that if today we were to write about someone like King Henry VIII of England, surely a lot of what we would have to say would be guesswork and conjecture."

"Yes, Philip, this is true in many ways. The description of the teacher you speak of and ask of was described in a very different way to how he was in reality."

"In what ways, Paul? Tell me what he was really like."

"You must understand, Philip, that I am from the very higher realms and know that Jesus of whom you ask was one of us. His work in your world was the combined inspiration of us all though he singularly made the decision to be part of your world, and knew what was set before him."

"But still, Paul, tell me what he was like."

"He was like any other man. This was his choice. He came and lived and died a human life and he loved all. He was not judgmental and never insisted on others doing what he said. In truth, Philip, he gave them great wisdom and knowledge that left the choice to do or accept to others. That was part of their progression."

"Have we ever got near to being what he told us we should be in our world?"

"Yes. In the era you call the 'sixties,' many followed a life that would have pleased the Nazarene. Men and women loved each other and strove to stop war. Some of the very wise ones of the 'sixties' also understood that God provided all for them, that work was an entrapment."

"Paul, I think you are talking about hippies, aren't you?"

"Yes, that is true. But in truth, I also say to you that many who lived a life like that lived a life that was similar to the way Jesus did. Many of your religious leaders who preach do not even understand the concept of the man they profess to follow, never mind living a Christ-like Christian life!"

"This is difficult for me, Paul. You are saying a hippie is more spiritual than, say, a priest, for example?"

"In some cases this is correct and in simple words you ask who the Big Boss of all is. That essence would wish all to try to love each other and never to destroy each other, especially in the name of religion, which many in your world have done now and throughout history."

"So in a nutshell, Paul, would it be sacrilegious to describe Jesus in this book as the Big Boss?"

"No, it would not be sacrilegious, Philip, but you must

remember we are all part of the Big Boss, as you describe him, and your description of Jesus in that context as being part of that oneness, that complete perfection, is not unfounded."

CHAPTER 31

CONVERSATION WITH MAURICE

This communication with Maurice was on August 29, 1998, at 8:45 A.M.:

"Good morning, Philip, my name is Maurice. It is my wish to speak to you regarding the book that you and Hans Holzer are writing to give you information that may assist you in bringing that work into the public domain."

"May I ask you questions, Maurice?"

"You may if you wish, but you will find that simply what I say to you answers many of your questions without your having to ask."

"Thank you, Maurice."

"It is known to us over here, Philip, of your beautiful, open channel to the spirit world that is not the blessed gift of all, and there is the answer to a question for you: this is why so many of your mediums who do get through to our world link with those in our world but cannot give names, addresses, and places the way you can for some people."

"You say for some people, Maurice. I thought I had this ability for all people and had confidence in my mediumistic talents."

"So you should. But it is also a two-way thing; no, a three-way thing! Also remember that many who come to this world stay in the dream-like state, a time of confusion, if you like, and although this is often for only a very short time, for others it can be a longer period, and placement to a higher level of existence can be a difficult thing to settle into. Think once again, my son, of dreaming. You will know that dreams will relate to material, physical, everyday matters, perhaps to things that have happened in the recent past or are happening in your present physical life, or the dreams visually represent your hopes for the future. All of these things are in fact physical conditions, yet are activated and experienced in what can be extremely confusing, dreamlike states, or what you call sleep time. That is what first transition through higher levels can be like. Therefore, when some of your mediums link with people in our existence, is it any wonder that the messages they give back to their loved ones in your world are sometimes mixed up or confusing?"

"Yes, Maurice. Thank you very much. That makes great sense."

"However, Philip, always tell those in your world that if those they care for do not seem to communicate, even when an open channel from a very good medium is available, it is not that they do not love you and no longer exist. Our consciousness is very different from yours, and, as I have said, the examples of your dream state are very good examples for you to explain to people. Also, starting any new life is difficult. You never remember what your spark of life was when a sperm fertilized an egg and then for nine months that soul spirit was nurtured and then brought into your physical world. Think how much more complex and difficult the progression to our world can be."

"The only thing I would say to you, Maurice, and do correct me if I'm wrong, is that I have had situations where a person has passed over and then perhaps almost immediately, within days, I have linked them with their loved ones in our world. How can that be so then? Do I delude myself?"

"No, of course not, Philip. For some, their transition can be that simple and easy, and with a medium such as yourself, of course, that connection is possible. Everyone is different and their progressions are different pathways too, but when

eventually they do become accustomed to their new surroundings and life, and yes, I say life, a loss of memory that
may have been there quickly returns. Likewise, intelligence,
intellect, and the immediate fulfillment of pleasures will be
there for them, but always tell your people that they do come
back and many would wish to help, but it is necessary for
those on higher levels to slow their vibration speed. This must
be learned and remembered so they can instantly be reunited
with their loved ones in what is a lower level—your world."

"When you say 'to help,' Maurice, what do you mean?
Can you give me an example?"

"The example is in your world already, Philip. Let me ask
if you attended one of your universities or colleges in your
earthly life?"

"Yes, I did."

"When you were in your first level, were there some in
the fourth level who became your friends and helped you
with certain difficulties that you had not yet experienced or
learned?"

"Yes, in some cases."

"Were there not great professors who had interest in individual students although only in their first year rather than
their last year—they just seemed to know that some people
were special?"

"Yes, that's true."

"There is the example in your world, Philip, and it is no
different here."

"Maurice, as we speak, I can quite clearly hear you of
course, but others in this room would not. Why is that?"

"You ask me questions you know the answer to, Philip.
When we share words, you allow your thoughts and my
thoughts to blend together. You allow me and others in our
world the opportunity to move a little further along our progression pathway, but to still keep the connection with your
world to pass through knowledge to try to help people; or in
some cases, just to let those know, who are desperately wor-
ried about those they have lost, that they are all right. There
are also those in your world, Philip, who consult what you

would call fortune tellers, wanting to know what lies in their future. Know this, Philip: The true psychic or medium operates as the receiver between our two worlds. We have no wish to change your free will or to interfere with the progression paths set before you. Therefore, I tell you in truth, do not listen to fortune tellers. Listen only to the real mediums and psychics such as yourself when you wish to know of our world and what happens here."

"I know it is true what you say, Maurice, and yet I have always had an interest in all the things you might call new age, especially astrology. In my earlier years, and even now I will still look at a person's aura to read and see what I can get from it."

"That is acceptable. There are many things concerned with your life on Earth and the life of others that are to be clearly seen and explained by the energy and differing colors seen around the physical body. Of course, a sensitive such as yourself will clearly read people from such information. We are aware, on this side, of your great interest in earlier years of astrology. We see no conflict for you, for here may be an art form that shows the correct pathways to follow, and, perhaps, difficulties and good things that lie along the path of life in your physical world. But know and understand this, Philip: Your mediumship is, of course, of a higher level and more meaningful to the progress of those you help and serve in your world."

"Maurice, may I ask you a question? How do you talk to your friends and colleagues in your world?"

Maurice answered this question with a chuckle. "In the same way I speak to you."

"Is that sort of telepathically then?"

"Yes, that's a good example. But do you not practice such things in your world as well? You do know, Philip, but you just do not accept or recognize it."

"Can you give me an example?"

"Okay. Do your remember your dog, Tina?"

"Yes, of course I do. Are you telling me you know Tina?"

"You asked for an example, Philip. This is nothing more.

Did you not find with this dog that you would not have to speak out? That you did not have to say the words of instruction? 'Heel! Stay! Sit! Go there, do this,' etc. Could you not simply think these instructions and she would respond?"

"Yes, Maurice, you are right, absolutely correct. She did understand."

"That is the example for you then. Even in the mind of a simple pet dog you could communicate with her. How much more in your world could be achieved if you were to practice this gift? Unfortunately, in your world it is the doubters and those who say these gifts are not evidence of telepathy that rule the roost!"

"Yes, I accept what you have given me, and thank you for the wonderful examples. I will teach them to my students. May I ask another question? What is it like for you in your world, and is there anything above that?"

"Many from your world and many from my world ask the same questions. Others have told you that when you come to our world everything you want is there for you. I can say no more than this is the truth. But there are higher levels of which I know no more than you know of our world, and there are people in these worlds that have greater knowledge and understanding than any, either of your world or mine. It is true to say I feel that some of your great film producers and writers have received inspiration from these levels, a glimpse or interpretation of thoughts from a higher source, if you like, with regard to what could perhaps be future experience, developments in your world or things that are available on a higher level. Even our world is very difficult to describe for you and for you to understand. Therefore, even more difficult to describe are those who exist in more progressed levels still. So, is it possible to describe them? Only by making progression to these levels will it become clear.

"Occasionally a few from your world do get to the gate, the pathway between your world and mine, if you like, and may get a glimpse of one of our other levels, and upon their return say it is so beautiful they cannot describe it in words, and they claim they come back with special abilities. I am not sure this is so but certainly they would come back to your world with more wisdom for they have sampled something wonderful. You in your world, Philip, must accept that you are on the steps of a great ladder that leads towards God, or the Great Boss you have asked us about. You are climbing towards a purpose or mode of creation, for us all, of complete oneness. Many in your world wish to know things you cannot possibly understand until you make your progressions. You look to the sky and see objects flying there that are not of your world; crops in the fields that are set out in special patterns that have no meaning to you. These things are complex and difficult for you to understand. But I tell you, Philip, we in our world are given even greater mysteries we do not understand and have to try to solve on higher levels."

"You evade my question, Maurice."

"I evade not, Philip! I tell you the truth."

"Maurice, what is God?"

"God is love."

"Is God a person?"

"God is both an infinite intelligence and perfect love."

"Can we communicate with God?"

"Every thought communicates with a higher source. As I have told you, in our world we have to rely on telepathy to communicate, and many try to send through thoughts of love, peace, and goodwill to those in your world, but in many cases it goes unrecognized the same as if you tried to send your own thoughts, Philip, to someone telepathically who had closed his mind. You would have had more success communicating with your dog, Tina. Do you remember what I told you? There are some who are afflicted as though they were deaf to any good words, including the thoughts of God."

"Maurice, when you speak of flying objects and patterns in fields are you referring to flying saucers and crop circles?"

"Those could be examples, Philip, but I can also only tell you what has been passed down to me. For these things you describe come from phenomena created from higher sources than the world I come from, higher levels of understanding. As to who is doing this, I do not know."

"Maurice, as I understand it, when we experience the different levels, we have come through a process of throwing off or discarding many different bodies and eventually become an energy source. Is this true? And if so, how can we still be the individual self if we are just energy?"

"Philip, I must remind you that physically we have lots of different features that allow others to recognize you—your face, the way you speak, your height, your body weight, and all the other things that are individual to you. All those who come over into our world bring with them an etheric duplicate of that earthly body, so, of course, are easily recognizable to everyone who would have recognized those things. The mind can manipulate and make the etheric body presentable at any age and time it would wish, and to be easily recognized. Yes, eventually you do become only pure energy, but individuality will always remain, ultimately moving towards a whole being. We're back to God again, aren't we!"

"Maurice, may I ask a few more questions?"

"Certainly."

"I take it that reincarnation is the truth as my evidence seems to overwhelmingly prove its existence?"

"Yes, of course it is the truth."

"Do men always come back as men and women as women?"

"It depends on what they need to learn, to progress."

"Why do people always seem, when they have knowledge of past life experience, to come from a different sort of tradition? For example, people who live in the Western world always seem to relate to India or North American Indians or civilizations such as that. Wouldn't it be fair to say if they had lived in our Western world they would have gained great wisdom and understood technology better than they did in an underdeveloped country?"

"That is true, Philip, but also remember that there is much to be learned from all types of existence. The Western world may be more technologically advanced and have material wealth, but is it more advanced in its natural wisdom or spiritual understanding of the existence you operate within? Of course technically the Western world has advancements over the poorer places in your existence, but it may be that the old Indian fakir has more knowledge to help and progress you than the Harvard professor. Those in your world should think wisely about what I have said to you, Philip, for that is also a great part of progression and understanding."

"Maurice, many have told me, in earlier communications, that when we pass over we go to different levels of existence, and that I can be with my wife, mother, father, and all the friends I have known in my earthly life. I trust that this is true."

"Yes, of course, Philip, this is true. I will not greatly expand on information that has already been given to you with great clarity from others; But one point I do have that may not have been presented to you before is the fact that not only will you meet the loves of your present life, but all the loves from previous lives. Give great consideration to what knowledge I present before you, Philip, which will be the most important wisdom you will receive. You will not know that until you have made progression to a higher level of your existence. Love and friendship and the incarnation you have now are restricted and have many limitations placed upon them. When you make your first progression above where you are now, certainly you can be with those you love or knew in your present existence any time you wish; but equally as important, you will wish to be with others who have come from other incarnations. This is the truth."

"Maurice, just one more question. It is my understanding that you are on a level above us and that there are many different levels Do you have birth and death in the way we know it?"

"Birth is the transition you make from all other levels, and all come over to us the way they were in the physical body. Death in your world is rather like etheric death in ours; it requires a type of rebirth. It is only the movement to a different level of existence. Really there is no death, only transition from one level to another. On my level of existence there are those who fear birth, or should I say rebirth, far more than people on your level fear death and their progression into ours in the etheric worlds. In truth, you should not fear death for it has no meaning, for there is no such thing. Life is eternal, and with that, Philip, I must wish you goodbye."

"Thank you very much for that communication, Maurice. Goodbye."

CHAPTER 32

A TALK WITH THE SPIRIT SARAH

This communication with the spirit Sarah was received on September 7, 1998, at 9:45 A.M.:

"Good morning, Philip."

"Good morning, Sarah."

"Philip, would you like to ask me some questions?"

"I would, Sarah. As I have asked all the other people from your world, I would also like to ask you what is it like for you?"

"Everything is perfect and as I would wish it to be."

"Sarah, apparently, once we come to a higher level of existence, we discard our physical body and turn into energy and light. Is that true?"

"Yes, that is so."

"May I ask you then, Sarah, how is it possible to retain our individual characteristics if we are just energy and light?"

"There is a simple answer to your question. In your world there are many characteristics and features that make you instantly recognizable to your loved ones and friends. Your face, the color of your eyes, the way you speak, the way you move, and all manner of little differences that make you what you are. As others will have told you, when you first come to our world, you come over exactly as you are with all these things. I must tell you, in our world energy and light are very different—a completely different frequency from that in which you exist. Our light is very intense, yet very beautiful and radiant. The personality of each individual is retained and shown by the shades and brightness of their spirit light. In these realms, people will recognize you, not by how you would physically look, but by the glow light of your spirit. Your individual personality traits will always still be there, but with time, they are less important and gradually fade."

"Sarah, is it true that in your world colors are different? It has often been said to me they are much more beautiful and bright."

"Philip, everything is as you would want it to be, but I do understand the question you have put to me. You must remember that all color and shade in your world are made from the light of your physical sun, and some things in your world more easily absorb the colors of your spectrum as you understand it. In the spirit world there are similarities. However, we do not have the physical sun as you do to provide light, but as you spend time on each level, moving towards oneness, so the light on each level gets brighter and more beautiful. This is why you have been told that our colors are more beautiful and, indeed, brighter than those in your world. In truth, this is only really on levels where those of a higher progression have come to. The light on the second level of existence above your world is a perceived thing of your own understanding and is very much the same as in your physical world, though of course your perception of this is more spiritual, and the lights and colors could seem brighter. In truth, for those in the transitional world, the first level, where those you consider to be bad go, there is very little light at all because the spiritual light they generate is so very dim, the colors, as you understand them, cannot be seen at all. Therefore, it is important for you to understand that when your friends from our level of existence communicate with you through your mediums, and speak of colors and light, you must appreciate it very much depends which level they exist on."

"Excuse me, Sarah, but could you clarify even further about the light? You tell me that there is light in the spirit world, and I think I understand some of the points you have put to me, but basically how can it be without a sun?"

"I will explain again to you, Philip. I do not speak of physical light, but the light that is created by the inner spirit, the higher mind essence, which creates all. Think of when you dream. Usually you dream only at night when it is dark. Do the dreams not usually seem to take place in areas that quite clearly have light? Think of it in simple terms, Philip. The Sun, which is physical in your' sky, sends down light vibrations, but your awareness of that light is only there when the light hits some physical part of your world. The light itself is invisible to the physical eye isn't it? Our world, the spirit world in its wider context, is made up of etheric things all of which vibrate on a much higher level than those you see within the light source that comes from the Sun. That is why the lights are brighter with each level of progression; the higher you get the more light there is.

"The second level of the spirit world is on a higher vibrational state than your world, so of course it is much brighter. There are those who have seen what can be described as ghosts or spirits (I do not like the word ghost, Philip, but I give it to you as an example for you to present in your book). Sometimes, the bright lights people see that look like figures or shapes, are individuals with an ability and psychic sensitivity among those in the etheric world who have glimpses of our world. I cannot make this any simpler for you, Philip, for it is not simple, it is complex. The intensity of light in our world is related to the spirit of the individual and which level they are operating on or attuning to."

"Sarah, will you tell me something of your life and your other lives?"

"No, not really, Philip, I can't see any benefit in that really. So many have already told you of experiences in your world and what they do in our world that my experiences are not of any real importance to you. You only ask, really, out of interest."

"No, I ask because I feel it would be interesting to the readers of our book."

"There are many who have spoken enough on the subject."

"It seems to me you don't really have any interest in the other lives you have lived, Sarah. Did you spend time in our world?"

"Of course."

"Do you have regrets in your world from when you were in ours, Sarah?"

"Everyone who comes up and makes progression from your world does, Philip. There are several words that come to mind: 'but' and 'if only' are a few! Always those who come to our world say, 'If only I had done this . . . I would have been kind to . . . If only I had known how . . . was suffering I would have helped them. . . . If only I had known how much . . . cared for me I would have been nicer to them. . . . If only I had known how poor people were in other parts of the world I would have helped them.' But you have to understand that if you did not have the progression to make you understand these things then that is part of the life you live and invariably when you come over to us you will have regrets."

"So are you saying to me, Sarah, that these things have to be, that you have to have an understanding of disappointments to progress?"

"Yes, that is so, Philip. And I will tell you that you need to have progression of past, present, and future for all are surely meant to be. If, in your world, you had the understanding of these three different areas, I feel you would quickly see no meaning to your life, especially your earthly life, and perhaps not even our realms. It is often told to us by our wise ones that to develop our mind and spirit we must continue to learn and progress. Certainly those of us who live our lives on the levels above you and who are still in a position to communicate in your world do not have the wisdom or knowledge to give you the answers to the mystery of life and creation itself. Wise ones that do, I tell you in truth, are on a much higher level than I am in many ways. The great Isaac Newton and my friend, Albert Einstein, discovered much and gave you knowledge and wisdom years before their time, and only now, in the spirit world, do they realize how much they were helped from this side in the presentation of their theories. Yet both have progressed by having to realize that many of their theories they believed came from their own physical minds were actually given them by great scientists who now reside in the spirit world. I know my message to you is short, Philip, but I am afraid that is all I can give you."

"No, Sarah, thank you very much for the wisdom you have brought for me."

"One other point before I go, Philip. Speaking in terms of time on our level, maybe I can give you a simple and basic understanding of how it operates here, again through the example of dreams. A dream may appear to last for hours, days, or even weeks, and yet has been proven through scientific research to last only seconds in your physical existence."

"Yes, I understand that to be the truth, Sarah."

"So understand when someone comes to our world, Philip, they may still be in a condition similar to your dream-like state, when perhaps in only hours they wake up and for a while believe they have covered the experience of days, months, and years. Sometimes, new spirits to our world have a similar experience as they adjust to their new world. Indeed, many years may flow by in your time in what may only seem seconds in our time. This is why sometimes people cannot understand why it takes so long for someone they love to contact them from the higher realms such as level two. Goodbye, Philip."

"Thank you, Sarah. Goodbye."

CHAPTER 33

MESSAGE FROM MICHAEL BENTINE

This communication with Michael Bentine came on September 17, 1998, at 3:45 A.M.:

"Good afternoon, Philip, my name is Michael Bentine."

"Good afternoon, Michael, it is good to speak with you again."

"Philip, I am very grateful for the help you gave to Clementina, also the help you give to Hans."

"I don't really know if I did help your wife, Michael. I gave her what you told me to say, but I didn't give family names or mention you as I felt this would be inappropriate with someone as famous as yourself, and I am sure with Hans, it is he who helps me rather than I who help him."

"That is not true; no one has helped Hans more than you have, Philip. Accept his compliments. I assure you he would not give them to you if you did not deserve them. Be assured he is not that sort of man. Also, you did help Clementina and you will help her in the future."

"I will certainly try, Michael."

"For now I am going to try to help you and Hans with this book. You want to know what the spirit world is really like?"

"We do very much. We think this might be a book that would help people."

"Then ask your questions and I shall tell you as much as I am allowed to."

"Michael, what I would like to do is ask you about your life, the type of existence you have now in the spirit world. Can I do that?"

"Yes, of course."

"Tell me about your passing over, Michael, and the people that you met when you reached the spirit world."

"Well, Philip, I had been ill for quite a long time and I was very weak. Therefore I had to spend a fair bit of time to recuperate, and even now it is very difficult for me to come back, even through the most open of mediums. That is why Clementina has not received the message that she wishes from me. But I shall break the code and she will see me."

"I told her that you stood by the head of her bed, and she told me she felt that."

"Good, thank you very much, Philip. Going back to what you asked me. Of course, I have many loved ones in this world who were waiting to take me over. You know, of course, about the terrible loss of my children. They were very quickly there for me."

"Yes, a lot of that was in the papers, Michael. Your son Stuart, and Mary, wasn't it?"

"By Mary I think you mean Marylla, Philip, but we called her Fusty, and Stuart, Gus; but actually it was my mother, Ma, who took me over and to a place of healing, rather like the hospital you know on Earth, Philip, where another dear family friend took care of me and gave me the finest nursing you could ever imagine."

"May I ask who that was Michael?"

"Ask Clementina, Philip, that will be a good link for you."

"All right, I will do that. Are you well now? Are you better?"

"Couldn't be better, Philip; absolutely perfect!"

"Good. So what are you doing in your everyday life, Michael? Are you still an entertainer?"

"Yes, but I am also doing much work between our world and yours, bringing about the awareness you and Hans work towards. Although I consider Hans to be one of my greatest friends, the book that you and he are writing will only be the starting point of real information coming through."

"That doesn't sound too good for us, Michael. Are you saying that Hans and I will get things started and then everyone else will bring it through?"

"The book is important, but, as you say, it will be the start of a floodgate in the time that you and Hans live."

"The last time I spoke to you, Michael, you told me something to say to your wife. You showed me something like a large piece of wood that you were blowing. What did that mean? What was the symbolism of that?"

"Again, you would have to ask Clementina, or possibly Hans. He would understand that. Yes, ask Hans Holzer."

"You know, you're not telling me too much today, Michael."

"I'm sorry, my boy! What else would you like to ask me?"

"One more thing before we start. The last time I spoke to you, you told me of working with a man called Jack. Who is he?"

"Yes, I was probably speaking of my cousin, John. Actually, he was the fellow who caused me to have a great love of airplanes and ended up in the RAF."

"No, Michael. You spoke of someone called Jack, not your cousin John."

"Yes, yes, of course. Jack is actually a man called Jack Hilton, the friend of a man I am doing a lot of work with now, someone who originally came from quite close to the area in which you live."

"Who would that be then, Michael?"

"A man called Tony Hancocks, a brilliant man."

"Oh yes, of course, I remember Tony Hancocks."

"I'm also working with Jimmy Edwards."

"So it's still all comedians together then, Michael."

"I suppose it always would be for me, Philip. I will tell you something you would not know and something others would not know either. When I was a little boy, I was very shy. That was why I always acted as the clown, and show business gave me the opportunity to always be the joker, so to speak; but the shyness always remained. Ask those who loved me and knew me best."

"Tell me more of what you do in the spirit world."

"Well, I work with people I would have admired when I was in your world."

"Really, Michael? Do you really do that?"

"Yes, of course."

"Can I ask you the sort of people you are talking about?"

"People like Laurel and Hardy, and Charlie Chaplin, and my great hero, Buster Keaton. But you know, Philip, and I do say this with a degree of pride, they tell me they admired my work from above as well! That makes me so very proud."

"So those above are aware of us below. They can see what we are doing—am I clearly correct on that?"

"Oh, yes, yes, of course. But you down below don't know of us unless you have a medium between the two worlds to communicate, like you, and tell them of the things we do."

"So what is your main project now? What are you doing?"

"I'm writing lots of things and producing lots of work. In our world you only have to think of something and it's there for you, so with the kind of mind I have, which, don't worry, is still there and that I still possess, this is a wonderful place for me. Many times, when I lived in your world, I would just think of something and wish I could do it there and then. But physically, you have to go get props and make things and then present it. Here it is done in a second. But for all the work that I do, it's basically just the same type of occupation I had in my earthly life because that's the work I love. I still have an interest in the paranormal, especially higher things above the level I'm on. See, Hans, I do not change, do I?"

"What level are you on, Michael?"

"Don't be silly, Philip, you know very well what level I'm on—level two."

"So you're trying to investigate the levels above you?"

"Well, I'm certainly trying to draw back the veils, to coin a phrase! If you tell Holzer I said that, he will know it's me. Always trying to draw back the veils, Hans, my old friend, to see what's above us!"

"I will pass that on, Michael."

"As you know, Philip, I have not been over that long, and the links are still very weak. However, I will always communicate and get back to you whenever you open yourself and are willing to help us, on this side, to help those in your world. As I say, I am fairly weak at the moment and can really answer no further questions, but I do wish both you and Hans good luck with your book. I would wish you to pass on one message to my fans who still live in your world and that is: know that life does still go on and death is not the end. Those who are in their darkest hour when they lose someone they love, especially a child (nothing is more difficult than the loss of a child), know that the child or person still carries on in a higher realm and that you will be together again in the spirit world. Also tell the partners who have been left behind by loved ones that life goes on and you will be together again. The human race lives forever. Philip, with that I must say goodbye to you."

"Thank you very much, Michael. That was a lovely communication and I do hope you will get back to me again when perhaps you feel stronger and can link with me more strongly. Goodbye."

CHAPTER 34

CONVERSATION WITH
MARLENE DIETRICH

This communication with Marlene Dietrich came on September 19, 1998, at 9:30 A.M.:

"Good morning, Philip. My name is Marlene Dietrich."

"Good morning, Marlene. It is very nice to speak to you."

"It is very nice to speak to you also, Philip. How may I help you?"

"Well, I don't know, Marlene. I was going to ask you the same question. Naturally I assume you have come through in connection with the book Hans and I are writing."

"Yes, I am aware of that book and I do think it is something that is very important for I feel it will help people not to waste their lives in your world."

"Surely you didn't waste your life though, Marlene. You must have had a wonderful life being such a famous lady, film star and what have you."

"You may say that, Philip, but I also realize I could have done so many more things with my life if only I knew then what I know now."

"What do you know now, Marlene, that makes you feel this way?"

"I know now that life goes on, Philip, that all the horrible things that happened in my life on Earth were all part of learning and preparing for where I am now."

"Horrible things . . . what do you mean?"

"Well, Philip, I will tell you in truth, despite what people may think, I was very lonely in my life and had to stay in your world for ninety-one years."

"You mean you died when you were ninety-one, Marlene?"

"Yes, yes, though I am surprised you use that word!"

"Yes, I am sorry, Marlene, passed over at ninety-one then."

"And I tell you, Philip, I was never really that happy. Even as a young girl I felt people used me, and I lived in the world when it was a terrible place, not a wonderful place. A place where war and evil were there, and in the last twenty years of my life I was very lonely, almost a recluse, if you like."

"Really, Marlene, were you?"

"Yes, Philip, I would not let people speak to me, not even accept that I was who I was, and I do regret that, for so many people did reach out to me but I would not reach back to them. There are very few photographs of me in the latter years of my life, I can tell you!"

"Is that so, Marlene? I didn't know that."

"You are writing this book with Hans Holzer. Give him my regards."

"I will Marlene. Did you know him then?"

"I have always been aware of Hans' work, and he helped an actress I admire and like, Elke Sommer, with a problem in the past."

"In what way did he help her?"

"Don't ask questions about other people!"

"Sorry, Marlene, I did not wish to offend you."

"You do not offend me, but I get easily bored."

"Okay. Tell me more about your life in spirit."

"No. I will tell you more about my time in your world if you don't mind, for that is where many lessons are learned to prepare you for this world. The last few years of my life were not pleasant and I was certainly not happy in my little apartment in Paris at the end of my days. Men in your world, young handsome people like you, Philip, also caused me many difficulties. No, women are much better; I preferred women in your world.

"Er, do you mean sexually, Marlene?"

"I speak of love, Philip. Yes, I preferred the love of women. Men could be marvelous when they wanted you, yet cruel when the need had passed. Women love more."

"I am sorry about that, Marlene."

"Why should you be sorry, Philip? All men are the same."

"I don't think I am, Marlene!"

"Maybe not, who can say? Even your co-writer now looks for love in his life, does he not?"

"You mean Hans?"

"Yes, yes."

"Do you know Hans, Marlene?"

"I didn't say that, but I know of your work with him."

"Marlene, I wouldn't want you to think I am being rude, but I would like to know more about the spirit world because that is what we need to know more of, and although I am fascinated by your earthly life, I really do need to know more of the spirit world."

"Yes, and those in your world all need to know more of the spirit world. When I was alive, I never believed in this spirit world that is now here for me. I always thought that when you died that was it. You would go into the ground and you would be finished. I was very wrong, I am glad to say!"

"Marlene, I don't want you to think I am pressing you again, but tell me of the spirit world. What are you doing now?"

"I am sitting with your friend, Elvis Presley."

"Marlene, I think you are joking with me."

"No, I am not!"

"Okay, then, can you describe the place that you live in now? Tell me what it is like."

"I have a beautiful, elegant apartment, nothing like the one where I spent my last days in Paris. It has many beautiful windows and a glass roof. When I look out of the window I can see a beautiful river, and I have maids here to attend me in much the same way they would have in my earthly life. And I have many friends."

"You know, Marlene, that sounds like a very material place you have. Would you describe it as being like that?"

"Oh, no, no, it is very spiritual. But in truth, Philip, I never believed in an afterlife. Also, in my earthly body for many years I had difficulty with my nasal passages and breathing, and also a problem with my leg and my back. None of these things are there now. I am in perfect physical health."

"Marlene, can I just stop you there and ask you something? If you are now in perfect physical health, then you are obviously not like the person you were when you went to spirit at ninety-one."

"Of course not. If you were to see me now you would see a young woman of perhaps twenty-six or twenty-seven. I am beautiful! I sing like an angel! Is that not true, Elvis?"

"Marlene, I think you are having a little joke with me from the spirit world. Is Elvis really there? Can I speak to him?"

"No, my dear, he is too fascinated with me to speak to you today! People love me in this world, Philip. That is what I always wanted. I wanted to be loved, and now in this world I can have all the things I wanted just by thinking of them. When I was twenty-six in your world if I wanted someone I would have that someone and in this world I shall be no different. Do I sound like a scarlet woman to you, Philip?"

"I wouldn't like to comment on that, Marlene, but you have given me a chance to ask a question. Let me ask if someone wanted a sexual relationship in the spirit world, would that be possible?"

"Of course, Philip, anything is possible, but there is more love here also. Huh! Sex without love. Love without sex. It should never exist. It should not be. Sometimes we take it, for that is all there is for us."

"Marlene, can I ask you how you talk and communicate with each other in the spirit world? We must get this properly understood for this work."

"The way I talk to you now, if I choose, but also we may

communicate by thought or telepathy. All I have to do is send my thoughts towards another and they are there."

"Are you working in the spirit world, Marlene? Does your career go on?"

"Of course, I am appearing in Elvis's production."

"I have a funny idea, Marlene, that you know I communicate with Mr. Presley, and I feel you are joking with me."

"I do not, Philip; I do not joke with you! When you speak to Hans you will know of these things."

"Come on, Marlene, tell me more about what the spirit world is really like. I want to know."

"It is exactly the same as it is in your world, except that whatever we want is there. When we think of it we can have it. But people are not so demanding over here. They accept you for what you are and you have the opportunity to progress and be the real you. In your world, people only want the image of me to be what they imagined I was, not what I really am. My fans wanted to possess me and, yes, you can tell my fans I loved them as much as they loved me."

"There are still many who love you now, Marlene. You are still a massive name in our world."

"Thank you, my dear! Thank you, my darling! Know that I also love you and them. Tell those that knew me in my latter years that I have my beautiful blonde hair again, and that I walk straight and confidently, and that I still love all—men and women—but that I have quickly come to learn in this existence that it is love that creates everything, not material things. You ask me what my world is like here, and I tell you in truth, Philip, it is the world I had on the earthly plane when I was twenty-six or twenty-seven; but I am surrounded by love, pure love. *Auf Wiedersehen*, my darling. Good luck and goodbye."

"Thank you, Marlene. I would have liked to know more of the spirit realms though."

"I have told you everything there is to be told. This world is no different from your world. *Auf Wiedersehen*."

"Goodbye, Marlene."

CHAPTER 35

ADOLF HITLER SPEAKS

This communication with Adolf Hitler took place on September 20, 1998, at 7:45 P.M.:

"Good evening, Philip. My name is Adolf Hitler, German Führer."

"I will answer you, Mr. Hitler, and yet say to you that I do not really wish to communicate with you."

"But you have communicated with me before, Philip. Did I not speak to you in the dream state?"

"You did, but I would repeat that I do not really wish to communicate with you."

"Did I not treat you with respect?"

"You did, Mr. Hitler, yes, and I found you a very reasonable man to speak to, but dreaming and communicating in this way are two very different things."

"Will you not give me the same respect and opportunity that you have given to others?"

"I will, but I must warn you that there are many that are close to me who would not wish me to speak to someone with the history and background of yourself; and I feel quite sure that my friend, Hans, will not publish your words and it will not be included in our book."

"Nevertheless, I will have my say, Philip. There are those who will tell you I was evil in your world. I was no more evil than many other people. There are those who will tell you I killed millions of people. It is not true. It was not my fault. Others told me that things were necessary. You must remember, Philip, that I did not come from an academic background. Like many other young German men, my education was not as it should have been. I fought in the First World War and then entered a manual trade. Foolishly, I listened to others who realized I had a magnetism that would be attractive and a powerful thing they could use."

"Can I stop you there for a minute, Mr. Hitler? Do you not accept that you were responsible for the countless murders of innocent people in the concentration camps?"

"I do not accept that I was responsible. It was others who were responsible. It was their fault, not mine."

"But you were the leader, you were in charge!"

"Why will you not accept it was not my fault? I was not responsible. I did not know these things were happening and though many in the West will tell you I did, I did not know they were happening!"

"Do you deny that you had a hatred of people because of the color of their skin, their religion, or what they were?"

"I hated all whom I thought stopped my people, the great German people, from progressing to their rightful place as leaders of the world. I still believe that. I still love the German, Aryan people, but I am sorry for the things that have happened and that I have been blamed for. I am sorry for these things. There are many mediums in your world who claim they have communicated with me. They have not. Only you so far."

"Did you not also create a war upon the Western world?"

"I did not! I took back what belonged to Germany that had been taken away unfairly, and other nations declared war on us; but again, I am sorry for these things and I am progressing in the spirit world."

"Can I ask you where you are? What level of existence you are on, Mr. Hitler?"

"I am on the first level of existence where many bad people are. I should not be with them. Very shortly I shall progress to higher levels, where my influences will be much stronger. I shall be able to come through to your world, and I will be able to explain things more positively. This time will come very shortly. It has taken me a long time to understand that I made mistakes, mistakes I am sorry for, but I will not be blamed for that which was not my fault. I wish to progress now and move to higher levels."

"Mr. Hitler, can I ask you a question that many people have asked over the years, and not really known the truthful answer to? Did you die at the end of the war or did you escape to somewhere else?"

"This is another nonsense that was told of my final days. I took my life when all was ended and nothing more could be achieved. Again, a grave mistake, but I shot myself and those I care for. I did not die in the cowardly way people will have you believe."

"Is that the truth, Mr. Hitler?"

"That is the truth, Philip!"

"And you are saying that you are now sorry for the things you did."

"I am sorry for many things I did in my life. I am sorry for all the mistakes I made, but I should not be blamed for all things. The Russians were to blame for many of the problems in the world, and many tell lies about me. I have come to you today to tell you of the world that I have existed in for many of your Earth years, and to warn others not to be evil or to follow bad pathways. For those who follow these ways in your world will come to a place that is, indeed, terrible, where you cannot have the kinship of the ones you love. For if they are good people, they will be in a higher level of existence; and for me, my life on this first level which is not that far from your own world, is often very dark."

"Do you associate with the devil, Mr. Hitler?"

"There are no devils as such on any of the levels. All have the devil within in all worlds, and even when I make my progression to a higher level, there are those who will find it difficult, even on the second level of existence, to accept me when I make my progression, the progression we must all make. I would ask that you tell all those in your world, your presidents, prime ministers, and those who are given power over nations, to think very carefully before they make decisions, that they not be tricked or deceived into doing bad things that other people would wish them to do so that history will show them blamed for all these things.

"Tell your leaders, tell your powerful ones, not to believe just because they are respected by people, because newspapers and the media present them as someone special, the gateways to the higher levels of existence will welcome them with open arms. They may not come to an existence such as the one I am in. When I first came here I still wished to carry on with war; I still wished to fight; even from this level I wished to influence my Aryan people to gain world domination. To accept their rightful place as leaders. There is a world that will accept such people. It is this first level of existence."

"What other people have come to that level that I would know of in history?"

"Great war leaders sometimes come here, Philip, and carry on with war. People who are only obsessed with making money and don't care for the Earth and cause upset for many people, sometimes come here. Murderers and very bad people come here. This is a place that can still have much violence and is very materialistic. It is a very sexual and sensual place, and I am ashamed to say that when I first came away from your world, I enjoyed this place. But that was many years ago and I now wish to move on."

"So you are saying you are sorry for your time on Earth and that you are also sorry for still being much the same when you arrived there?"

"It is difficult for me to accept that I am sorry, but it is as you put it. More learning about the things that are wrong and the things that are right. My message is that however bad you were on the Earth plane, there is an opportunity to progress and to move upwards."

"Mr. Hitler, I know this is a very difficult question, but I feel I have to ask it if we are to talk. Will you be reborn? Will you come back to this world? It is something that many people would fear."

"It is cruel what you ask me. Would you deny me rebirth?"

"I feel there are many who are the descendants of people who feel you have hurt them beyond belief who would deny you rebirth, yes."

"But what if I said to you, Philip, that the next time I came back I would be a completely different person? A person who would have nothing to do with war or killing. Would you deny me that rebirth?"

"I think there are people that would, Mr. Hitler, yes."

"Then you see they have things to learn themselves. Out of darkness cometh light, does it not?"

"It does, but there are many who are scared of the dark and what it might bring forth. I am afraid I can no longer continue with this communication. I am grateful to you for telling me what it is like in that first level of experience, and I thank you for that, but I now wish to end this communication."

"I agree to release you from this communication, Philip, but at some time in the future, you will act as my medium to tell the world the truth of the life and times of Adolf Hitler, Führer of the German nation. Goodbye."

CHAPTER 36

MESSAGE FROM BERNIE WINTERS

This communication with Bernie Winters, the great British comedian, came on September 23, 1998, at 8:45 A.M.:

"Hello, Philip."

"Hello, Bernie, how are you?"

"Very well. So you are going to write a book about the spirit world then?"

"Well, I'm trying, Bernie, but it really depends on Hans Holzer. He's the one who is so important with it. All I do is talk to people on the Other Side, and mostly people I don't know at that, or people like yourself, or people I've met occasionally. How are you, anyway?"

"Very, very well. Of course, I was very ill at the end of my life in your world. You know that, don't you?"

"Yes, so I believe, but you're fine now I take it."

"Yes, yes, absolutely marvellous."

"Is that always the case with someone who has been very ill, Bernie? Did you find that you were soon made better? Were you immediately okay?"

"I was still a bit frail when I first came over."

"By the way, what level are you on?"

"Oh, I'm definitely on the second level that people have talked to you about. Going back to what I was saying, of course I am much better now, but when I first came over I was rather weak and tired. But there are people waiting for you in places very much like the hospitals in your world, and you are quickly up and about and back to your normal self."

"So what are you doing in life, Bernie? Do you still do the same things that you did here?"

"Yes, I was always drawn to show business really, that was always what Mike and I wanted to do."

"Do you mean your brother, Mike?"

"Yes, he's in America now, you know. We split up in the late seventies, but we always loved each other. Bit of bad blood between me and Mike at one time, but everything's okay now. I always try to help him as much as I can and I know he always sends his thoughts to me as well. We're very close, Mike and I. If you ever see him, you tell him how much I love him."

"Of course I will, Bernie. You knew my friend as well, didn't you: Rustie Lee, the black comedienne?"

"Yes, of course, give her my regards. You don't ever see Sue Pollard, do you, Phil?"

"I think I have met her a few times, but no, I don't see her or know her well."

"Well, if ever you do, let her know I'm really grateful for the support she gave me in my darkest moments. She'll know what that means. Just tell her that."

"Yes, I'll do that for you Bernie, definitely. Tell me a bit more about yourself and specifically the spirit world if you can, and the things you do."

"Well, I was born in the early thirties, 1932, in a place called Islington."

"Yes, I know Islington quite well, Bernie."

"And they say I was the biggest baby they had ever seen, which is strange really because my mother, Rachel, and my father, Samuel, were both quite small. Perhaps they wondered where the genes came from, and I was certainly different from my brother. Mike was far more clever than me; he was always really clever. I also had a lovely sister, good parents, everything you could ask for really. Our real name was Weinstein, and Mum was always the boss of the family, always plenty to eat on the table, and the cleanest house in London. Eventually, Mike and I went into show business. We had a lot of family, you know, with boxing connections, like your family, Philip."

"Did you know that about me then, Bernie?"

"Yes, I wouldn't come and speak to you without checking you out first; don't worry about that, my boy!"

"That's very funny, Bernie."

"What's funny?"

"You saying you've checked me out. You know, making inquiries from the spirit world before talking to me."

"Oh, absolutely. We've got no time for fools on this side of existence, I can tell you that much! And you are very lucky to be working with Hans Holzer as well, because he doesn't suffer fools in your world either!"

"I'm sure you're right. He's a man I care very much for, Bernie, and I'm sure that's true."

"Anyway, into show business we went and we were all pretty good at it. My sister sang, my brother did impressions, and I tried impressions but quickly realized I would do better as a clown or a comedian. So that's what I did, and we entered a few competitions and won them, and eventually got some work. Then a guy called Johnny Riscoe helped us a lot really, an agent in London."

"I've heard that name before. That's Patsy Martin's father's name, isn't it?"

"Yes, that's right."

"She helped me a lot you know, Bernie. She's a really nice lady. At one time I was writing a book about boxing and she got the famous boxer, Henry Cooper, to do the foreword for me. A very nice lady."

"And Johnny Riscoe was a very good man as well, Philip. Crafty and a good businessman, but a bloke with his heart in the right place; and basically from there on we went into all sorts of different things and we ended up doing the Palladium, having our own show and nothing but success really. But eventually Mike and I split up and I worked with my dog, Schnorbitz, and that was another start to my career. I never made as much money as a lot of people thought though. Mike was the guy with the brains for making money, but I never went too short. But then I had what you would call a bad-luck go of it, and at fifty-eight I was finished in your world—cancer of the bowel."

"That was very unfortunate, Bernie."

"Well, it's what's meant for you, isn't it? And I'm happy over here. Course I miss Siggy, my wife, and my son, Ray, but I'm often back around your world and I'm never very far away from them. You can tell Siggy if you ever meet her, I've got my Roller over here, she'll know what I mean. I've got my Roller, and that makes me very happy—that and my golf."

"What other things do you do, Bernie? Do you still do the same work?"

"Oh, yes, of course. I mean it isn't a case now of actually playing Bud Flannigan; I'm actually working with Flannigan and Allen! And people like Tommy Cooper. I used to miss Tommy when I was in your world and he came over, but I'm doing a lot of work with him now."

"What sort of home do you live in, Bernie?"

"It's more of flat, really, that I live in and I'm very much involved in writing comedy now as well as acting it. I'm also writing a book about my life."

"You said you liked your golf and your car where you are now, Bernie, so are there roads there? Can you drive down highways and motorways and what have you?"

"Well, of course, Philip. You've already been told that anything you want here you can have, so they are here for me; and they've got some pretty great golf courses, I can tell you!"

"And your loved ones and friends, Bernie, are they with you?"

"We all have our loved ones, like our parents and partners, and, of course, one day I'll be united with my wife and my son and his family. We all come together eventually."

"And your friends?"

"Yes, and of course I've made lots of new friends as well."

"I'm trying to find out things, Bernie, so I can pass them

on to people so they have an understanding of what it's like. Why would you want a Rolls Royce in the spirit world?"

"Because I loved it when I was in your world and anything you want here you can have. I spent a lot of time driving a Granada Estate as well, which did the job, but I didn't love that like I did the Rolls Royce. So it is here for me, Philip. It's as simple as that!"

"Okay, would you like to come back in another life here at some time? Is that possible, Bernie?"

"Of course it's possible. You can come back and live lives again in your world, but that's not for me, not the essence of Bernie Winters anyway. Maybe something of my spirit will come back and progress, but I'm here for those that I love, and I'm waiting for those other people who love me in your world to be here with me as well."

"This may seem a funny thing to ask, but do you still make people laugh? Do you have big comedy shows in the spirit world? Some people might think it's a place that is very spiritual and that humor wouldn't be so abounding."

"Well, they would be wrong! It's full of fun. Think of all the great comedians who have come here. They don't stop their work just because they're in a different existence, Philip."

"You see, one of my problems, Bernie, is getting through to people what the spirit world is like."

"Well, you can't really. You can only tell them that we carry on, that we exist, that we are just the same as we were in your world. It's just another existence. Look, I was very poorly before I came here, and I very quickly decided that I didn't want to feel like that, the terrible pain and what have you, and I didn't want to look like that anymore. So I was helped to bring it into balance to get shut of it, to be cleared of it, and I feel just great. I came to one of the hospitals here where we have wonderful doctors and nurses. You have to learn to understand that it's a different way of life; although you can have everything physical if you want to, it is a spirit existence. I quickly accepted that and was just as quickly brought into balance. I'm learning a lot now about progression and understanding other things. I always loved German food, you know, and there are lots of German foods here for me.

"One thing you can tell people in your world who are very ill or sick and it seems as though they will be coming to the spirit world quite soon, is to stick with it, don't feel so bad. When you get here you will be quickly relieved of that pain. Everything about this world is good and pleasant and kind, and we'll quickly sort you out; and don't worry about dying either, because your mother or father or someone like that will be waiting at the side of your bed, and when you leave your physical existence, they will bring you over. No doubt about it. And perhaps the most important thing anyone can tell you about this existence is this spirit world is very similar to your earthly world, especially this second level of existence, which I'm in, and where most of the people you love and care for will come to. Anyway, that's about it. Pass on the word, everything carries on. Good luck with your book and as we used to say in show business 'break a leg.' Goodbye."

"Thank you for that, Bernie. Goodbye."

CHAPTER 37

MARILYN MONROE TALKS

This communication with Marilyn Monroe occurred on September 26, 1998, at 10:45 P.M.:

"Hello, Philip. It's Marilyn . . . Marilyn Monroe."

"Hello, Marilyn. How lovely to speak to you, again."

"Yes, many times we have spoken in the past, haven't we? So I'm not going to tell you about the things that happened in my life, because I've moved on and I've passed now, and it has no significance. So don't ask questions about what happened to me in the last few hours of my life in your world because it's not important, and don't ask me about any of my relationships or other things that happened to me in your world with men or anything. What I have come through for is to tell you and the people who will read the book about the spirit world, nothing more, nothing less!"

"Marilyn, that would be wonderful, really, because lots of celebrities have come through but they do reminisce a lot and talk about their life in the physical world, and it's not really what we want to know about."

"It's natural that they want to talk about physical things, Philip, because they are drawn back to your world. They have lots of memories and love in that world that draw their thoughts back, and when they speak to a medium like you, they can't help but reminisce, if you like."

"Yes, I can understand that, Marilyn. Actually, that's a good point!"

"I've got nothing at all that draws me back to your world. I was never happy in it. I am going to tell you about this world so that when people come over they are confident and don't need to worry about it, because passing over, dying, means nothing. It is just like stepping out of one set of clothing into another, it's as simple as that. All the wonderful things you would want in your life, and the way you would want people to be, and the way you would want to be treated are here for you."

"Is that the same for you, Marilyn?"

"Yes, of course it is."

"I'm glad to hear that."

"I am also a serious actress here, and training to be better. I also do loads and loads of work with little children. Lots of children are in this world, Philip, who were no more than sparks of life, who came up from your world and were aborted, miscarriages, and things like that, and they are such lovely little mites. I love to work and play with them."

"Did you ever have an abortion or miscarriage, Marilyn?"

"Now remember what I told you, Philip. I'm not going to talk to you about your world. I'm just going to talk about this world."

"Yes, you're quite right, that's great. Carry on, Marilyn. Tell me about the things you do."

"I do all the things that are wonderful. Things that I never dreamed I could do."

"Such as?"

"Well, I sing very well, and people treat me seriously, and I'm never sad because everyone loves me, especially the children. That's the work I hope to do in the future. It is my hope, Philip, to progress and reach higher levels and work with the mediums in your world like yourself."

"I don't think that's so special, is it? Almost anyone can do that from your world can't they?"

"Oh no, you are quite wrong. You have to have a reason for coming back whenever you do so. It has to be important."

"So what is the reason for you coming back and telling me these things?"

"Because people in your world think of me as an actress and celebrity, as someone special, although I'm not, but they will listen and accept the words of people they think of as celebrities in your world. Therefore, we have the opportunity to come back to influence and change, to see what your world is like now, and know it is a place of learning for us even now in our world."

"If that's the case, wouldn't you like to come back and live another life, Marilyn?"

"Oh dear me, no! Definitely not!"

"Do you have a relationship in your world, if you don't mind me asking, and can people have relationships?"

"Yes, of course they can."

"Like a physical one or a sexual one?"

"Yes, if that's what you want, but I've moved on from that as well. I'm spending a lot of time around Joe, mind you."

"Who's Joe"

"Joe DiMaggio, my baseball guy! Joe and me get on just fine, and he's the one who makes me really happy."

"So there is a man in that realm who is with you and you're happy together then, Marilyn?"

"Yes, but it's more of a love/best friend thing rather than a physical thing, really. That's the way I want to move forward. I want to learn all about these things and maybe come to do some work with the mediums of your world. That's probably the only way I would come back, like I am with you."

"It sounds to me as though you're already progressing, Marilyn."

"I would like to think so, Philip. I'm also working with a girl called Maureen Carr. We've helped some people who had some real problems and who have just come over. I will tell you, these days there are a lot of people who come to this world after committing suicide or perhaps having been murdered in your world."

"So are you aware of that happening in your world, Marilyn?"

"Well, no, we're not, but I'm sure a higher force is. When such people come to this world it is sometimes a bit of a shock for them and they need time to adjust, but with love and care and understanding it can be explained to them they have come to another place, that they are in another existence, and they quickly come to terms with their passing over."

"So you're almost like a spiritual welfare worker?"

"Yes, I rather like that, that's a good way of putting it! Me and Maureen are spiritual welfare workers, but we've had to work hard to get to that. It isn't easy. Some people come over from your world, like Princess Diana or Mother Teresa, and immediately fall into that way of working as part of their help and progression, but it's not so easy for some of us. I've had to work to get there, but I do feel I'm quite capable of helping lots of people who have had similar lives in your world to what I had."

"But wouldn't that have been a wonderful life, being a film star, Marilyn?"

"I had a terrible life. This is far better. Time means nothing. There are no restrictions on time. Sometimes we even lose it a little bit and can spend days just drifting, relaxing, and absorbing this wonderful atmosphere. Other days we are far more attuned to things, like I am today with you. But I don't have to be. I can just float and relax and absorb the beautiful vibrations that are all around me."

"So you can make time for yourself and time can be how you want it to be, Marilyn?"

"It is no different from anything else in this world, Philip. Anything you want can be as you want it to be. It is strange in your world, how people suffer when they have terrible illnesses and hang on to life, and yet the minute they see the light of the spirit world, they are drawn towards it and they never want to come back, you know, except to progress at later times, and to try to move to a higher level of existence. But there are people in your world who know the name 'Marilyn Monroe' and would listen to me and associate it with the things I did in your world and perhaps listen to me; and if they would, you tell them, Philip, that they have nothing to fear in death. Death may hide us but it never divides us. We are just a step beyond, and when your time comes, you, too, will be part of this wonderful spirit world.

"Thank you, Philip, for letting me speak, and good luck with the book. With all of us showbiz guys and gals communicating with you I bet they will call you the psychic to the stars. And it looks like I'm still topping the bill over here, doesn't it!"

"Yes, it looks that way! Thank you very much, Marilyn."

CHAPTER 38

CONVERSATION WITH DANNY KELLY

This additional information was received from Danny Kelly on September 28, 1998, at 9:00 A.M. I asked for it following a fax from Hans in the early hours of the morning:

"Good morning. My name is Danny Kelly. I am allowed to come through to you to help with Hans and your book."

"Thank you very much, Danny."

"Well, Philip, I had many difficulties."

"By that, I take it you mean in my world, Danny?"

"Yes, over there I was gay, and for my family, it was very difficult for them to accept."

"I see."

"But over here, things are so different. All are accepted and in this realm of enlightenment, everything the individual would want his or her existence to be likeis the way it is."

"But, Danny, being gay is accepted here as well now, isn't it?"

"You're joking, aren't you? It is still Hell before coming out, and even then in living your life, in your world, being different is not easy. Someone with your sensitivity knows that quite well."

"Yes, I suppose I would accept your view. But you must see, Danny, it is not part of my life so I don't understand it."

"Exactly! You have to feel the pain of things to understand

them, don't you? But you have a lot of friends who are gay, don't you?"

"Oh, yes, it doesn't matter to me at all."

"Anyway, when a person comes over here, everything and everyone is accepted."

"One point, Danny: almost every religion rejects homosexuality, doesn't it? How does that fit in with your world?"

"Religion doesn't rule our world, only one great Godhead that all of us are working towards together. We are helped to fit in and become part of everything that goes on. But it has happened in your world, hasn't it? Think of some Native American tribes if they had people who were different like us. An example being the Ponka tribe who let their gay guys, they call them the 'berdache,' wear dresses and were quite happy with it; and the same opportunities were there for their women also. But the berdache, for instance, still went to battle and helped the injured during times of war, and had other roles of importance in everyday tribe life. I have made a friend of a guy from that background who lived many years ago. You know, Philip, the Indian tribes were far more civilized and understanding than us in many ways."

"Yes, Danny, that's a good point. But let me ask you something else. Surely nature is heterosexual. If not, we would have no continuing life as we know it, and the human race would come to an end. Indeed, your spirit world is always telling me of the fact of continuing life hereafter."

"Yes, Philip, but there is room for all. You can only judge yourself and there are plenty of others who continue to bring life back into your world."

"Another question, Danny. There are men and women who feel they are gay but do not want to be. What happens to them?"

"Easily answered, Philip. In our world, you quickly become what you want and everything is there for you. Many have told you this. We are talking about your book over here you know. It is in our newspapers."

"You have newspapers and things like that then?"

"We have everything we had in your life, and so much more."

"Another question, Danny. What about bisexuals?"

"Again their existence here is what they wish it to be. But you do already understand, you and Hans, this is sometimes relevant to past life experiences, and gender insecurity can be a difficulty that was only faced in your world. Indeed, for some, even homosexuality can be an imbalance that can be quickly corrected and replaced by a heterosexual nature if it equals happiness for the individual. There is no hard and fast answer. The true answer is, as I have said, how you wish to be is how you will be in our world."

"Okay, tell me of your life in spirit."

"I am wonderfully happy and completely accepted for what I am. I like to wear ladies' and feminine clothes, very pretty things; so I do, and no one minds! I am also helping my dearest friend, Justin, who has just come over and is settling well in his new existence. You see, Philip, I am not alone. There are many like me."

"So is it a place just for gays where you are, Danny?"

"No, you misinterpret me. We are just accepted here. Not our own place though. We are still with all our friends and relatives who are heterosexual because we love them and they love us. One thing that may help you, Philip: a lot of gay people choose to come back to your world. Strange, considering the pain they have had, but feeling the need to see if they actually missed anything, and wanting the experience of heterosexuality. Some have found it a difficult thing. There are some in your world who have genuine femininity of the spirit, or masculinity, if they are lesbian. That's why some people in your world who are 'all man' or 'all woman,' to coin a phrase, feel they are most definitely the opposite on the inside. I must stress this is not the answer to all, mind, but it is the truth for some. Philip, tell your people to have understanding in their hearts, not criticism, of that which they do not understand. All are equal in the end. Indeed, I am told in the higher realms it is not a question of gender; we are both male and female."

"Now that is very interesting about the higher realms, Danny. Can you give me an example?"

"Not really, Philip, I am only just coming to terms with this world."

"Yes, okay, Danny, I understand that. May I ask how old you are and do you have a partner in your world? I presume that such a relationship would be accepted."

"In your years, I am about thirty-nine now. In my prime, if you like. Still good looking, but knowing the way of things. I do have a partner, but I will not give his name as I know his father will read this book and be offended by what his son was and is. (Strange that, Mr. X, isn't it, when you were a bit our way yourself? Yet you gave your son such a terrible life of feeling shame and not being what he should be. See, Mr. X, lessons are quickly learned for all here!) Anyway, Philip, my partner and I have a good time. Night club life is very important to us both, and we've got some good ones here. We both work together designing clothes, which was also our occupation in your world. Both of us are setting time aside, though, to attend one of our colleges, which are much the same as the ones in your world, by the way, because one day we hope together we will move to a higher realm."

"If I could just stop you there for a moment, Danny, which level are you actually on?"

"Level two of course! Where else?"

"Thank you, Danny. I just wanted to be sure of correct placement."

"Tell the people in your world, Phil, there are those who would have you believe that people like me and my friends go to bad places and that we are bad. This is not true. We are what we are and God, the higher realms, and the guides and teachers, love and care as much for us as for anyone else. Our time in your world was often made difficult by others who have a great deal to learn in their own individual progressions. Not so for a lot of us as we used much of our time there as a learning process. Now the spirit world, for us, is perfection itself. Others will have told you anything you want is there for you. Those who are like us in your world will know, one day, this same blissful acceptance of different people, and when their time comes to pass over they should not be afraid. The spirit world is a wonderful place which awaits all, whoever or whatever you are. Goodbye and thanks for talking to me, Philip."

"Goodbye, Danny."

CHAPTER 39

CONCLUSIONS BY
PROFESSOR HANS HOLZER, PH.D.

Had I not become totally convinced of the reality of Philip Solomon's ability to communicate with people in the world of spirit, this book would never have involved me.

For the first and only time in my experience as a psychical researcher, who neither believes nor disbelieves but searches out the evidence, the facts, I was confronted with massive evidence that could in no way be explained by any other means except that the living people in the world of spirit were in fact speaking to Philip, and vice versa.

Other mediums have brought me unassailable evidence of such communications before, but not on the scale Philip has done. Even the most skeptical scientist will agree that specific data given by someone who has no knowledge of them, no access to them in any way whatever, and communicated to someone who is equally ignorant of them—in this case myself—that such data cannot be explained in any other way than the way claimed, as genuine spirit communication between a discarnate, living person and a medium in our world.

If this be so, and I have long come to the conclusion that it is, we know a great deal more because of it; about what awaits all of us once we cross over into the next phase of existence, the afterlife.

Those are my scientific, reasonable conclusions, and they have nothing whatever to do with religion or belief. I think our religion, our faith, partake of an entirely different level of our personalities, and in no way replace or diminish a scientific attitude of acceptance regarding what is being reported in this book.

There are some peculiarities running right through all of the case histories reported by Philip Solomon. In essence, the world whence the communicators report is a world in which thoughts, desires, visualizations (that is, specifically programmed thought energy) take on three dimensional characteristics no different from what exists in our denser, physical dimension. Everything in the universe, or universes, has substance. Only the degree of solidity, the density of particles, differs between our denser world and the next.

When mediums visit in that world, the world of spirit, they do so, not with their outer, physical body, but with their inner, etheric body, the aura, where they "live" before and after death. When people from the spirit dimension enter our world they will be visible or audible to those whose etheric body, or aura, is attuned to them, which is a matter of random ability occuring to some people, and in varying degrees, but not to all. Hence the experiences of this kind are not unusual, but hardly common. That thought can create total reality is hardly new. Descartes taught that *"Je pense, donc je suis: cogito, ergo sum!"* which may be translated as "I think, thus I am" or, as I prefer, "As I think, so I am."

The nature of time is also puzzling as it is, of necessity, different over there. Time is a dimension connected to a three dimensional world. Time over there is not so limited, being an aspect of a different kind of world and dimension. But there is progress through developments from stage to stage, from consciousness expansion to the next, and we need to understand it better than we do so far. But judging from these protocols and similar reports from other reputable mediums, "the world next doors" as Eileen Garrett called it, is far from haphazard or subject to whims, special "deals," or the like. Above all, it need not be feared any more than being born into this world should be feared; nor, for that matter, death, as we know it—life's other door.

If our faith assumes that all comes from God, then it should surely include a universe where all is orderly, and where the transition from one energy level, the denser physical outer body, to a less dense level, the spirit body, is part and parcel of the system; or, if you prefer, of the Divine Will.

We are not here discussing the origin of the system, nor its hierarchy, but the fact of its existence per se.

With that, many who will read this book may experience a change of mind, of heart, about the very nature of their existence, and what awaits them beyond the physical state.

INDEX

Abraham, 41
accidents, death by, 20, 32
afterlife, 12, 14, 36
    perception of, 58–59
    See also spirit world
age, 57–58, 67, 110, 149
ancestors. *See* family
Anderson, Marisa, 7
angels, 51, 117–20
    guardian, 21–22, 119
    role of, 87–89
animals, 98
    See also pets
astrology, 170
aura, 170, 213
authority. *See* hierarchy, of spirit
    world

babies. *See* children
Beethoven, Ludwig Von, 18
Bentine, Michael, 181–85
birth, 56, 174–75
body, in spirit world
    appearance of, 23, 103,
        110–12
    awareness of, 21
    etheric, 3, 173, 213
books, 95–96
    writing, 145
Brown, Rosemary, 18

Caesar, Julius, 128
Capone, Al, 131–38
Carr, Maureen, 204–5

channeling, 10–11, 152–53
Chaplin, Charlie, 184
Cherubim, 118–19
children, 67, 98–99, 111, 203
    education of, 55, 161–63
Chopin, Frederick, 18
cities, 46, 61–62, 85, 146
clairaudience, 17–18
clairsentience, 17–18
clairvoyance, 17–18, 31
clothes, 103
colors, 31, 177
communication
    with extraterrestrials, 106
    between physical and spirit
        worlds, 3–4, 16–18,
        39–40, 45–47, 55–56, 147
    telepathic, 30, 66, 169–72,
        189–90
    See also mediums
consciousness
    cosmic, 41
    and dreams, 168
    levels of, 85
    survival of, 3, 12, 17
Cooper, Henry, 198
Cooper, Tommy, 199
Crazy Horse, 65
criminals, 38–39, 97, 100–102, 194
"A Crisis in Science" (*Life
    Magazine*), 4
crop circles, 172
crystals, 85
Custer, George, 64–65

dance, 93–94
David, 19–25
Davis, Jr.,Sammy, 92
Dean, James, 68
Dean, Stanley R., 2
Descartes, René, 213
desires
    fulfillment of, 31, 81, 115, 142,
        190, 213
    overindulging in, 99–100
Diana, Princess, 52, 71–75, 205
Dietrich, Marlene, 186–90
DiMaggio, Joe, 204
dimension(s)
    multiple, 1
    of spirit world, 36, 58
disabilities, 37–38, 59, 108
doctors, 56–57
Dora, Sister, 37
dreams, 168

Earp, Wyatt, 68
Earth
    nature of, 82
    protection of, 84
eating. *See* food
education, 64, 73, 78, 115
    of children, 55, 161–63
Edwards, Jimmy, 183
Einstein, Albert, 179–80
emotions, survival of, 79
    See also pleasure, survival of
energy, 85, 176–77
entertainment, 34–35, 44, 61,
        68–69, 91–94, 145–46, 200
evil
    source of, 104
    in spirit world, 66–67, 100–102,
        126–30, 193–94
evolution, 42
extraterrestrials, 106

facilitator, 162
faith, role of, 2
family
    reincarnation of, 111, 149–50
    reuniting with, 20–23, 27,
        80–81, 174, 182

Fate (magazine), x, 7
flowers, 94
Flynn, Errol, 68
food, 42–43, 60, 78
    meat, 98
form, taking, 19
Franz, 151–54
free will, 45, 49, 104–5
    and progression, 88
frequency, of spirit world, 58,
        148–49
future, seeing the, 83–84, 107

Gabriel, Archangel, 118
Gandhi, Mahatma, 52, 80
Garland, Judy, 139–43
Garrett, Eileen, 213
gender, 43–44, 87, 209
ghosts, 2, 101, 178
God, 41, 60–61, 87, 89, 153, 172
guardian angels, 21–22, 119
guides, 14, 20–22, 31, 49, 52–53, 152
    and mediums, 33–34, 55–56

Hancock, Tony, 183
Hardy, Oliver, 69, 184
Hart, Hornell, 2
healing, 20, 30, 56–57, 108, 115,
        200–201
    "healing houses," 28–29
    the physical body, 87
Heaven, 38, 41
Hell, 39
hierarchy, of spirit world, 47–48,
        60–61, 79–80, 153, 164–66
    and angels, 87, 117–20
Hitler, Adolf, 128, 191–95
home, 20, 23, 188–89, 199
homosexuality, acceptance of,
        207–11
hospitals, 56–57, 67–68, 80
Houdini, Harry, 69

illness, 28, 30, 80, 108
    See also healing
individuality, survival of, 21, 173,
        176
instruments, musical, 92

Jackson, Peter, 49–53
Janet, 54–62
Jenny, 160–63
Jesus, 41, 52, 60, 69, 118, 164–66
Joanna, 148–50
John, 97–108
Johnny, 155–59

Karter, Kathleen, 7
Keaton, Buster, 184
Kelly, Danny, 207–12
Kennedy, John F., 80
Kirlian photography, 3
Kübler-Ross, Elisabeth, 2

Larry, 90–96
Lassaw, Yolana, 5–6, 7
Laurel, Stan, 69, 184
learning. See education; universities
Lennon, John, 52
Le Shan, Lawrence, 5
Lewis, Richard, 42–48
library, 91, 94–95
life
    dualism of, 49
    force, 3
    on other planets, 86
    purpose of, 106
Life After Life (Moody), 2
light, 85, 176–78
Lincoln, Abraham, 80
Liszt, Franz, 18
Lodge, Oliver, 69, 158
love, 30, 79, 141
    and God, 172
    and mediums, 154
    and reincarnation, 174

Mabel, 109–13
marriage, 67
    See also relationships
Martin, Patsy, 198
Mary of Medici, 117–20
Maurice, 167–75
McIntosh, Don, 2–3
meditation, 154
mediums, 11–12, 17–18, 47, 56,
    153–54

Fate article, 7
    reliability of, 33–34, 152–53,
        167–70
    in spirit world, 79, 88–89, 108
    See also Solomon, Philip
Michael, 82–89
Michael, Archangel, 118
mind
    healing with, 108
    limits of, 17
    power of, 103, 213
Mollenhauer, Bernard, 4
Monroe, Marilyn, 68, 202–6
Moody, Raymond, 2
Moses, 41
Murphy, Gardner, 5
music, 44, 61, 92, 114

near-death experience, 123–24
Newton, Isaac, 179–80
nirvana, 40

occupation. See work
O'Kelly, Patrick, 26–29
On Death and Dying (Kübler-Ross),
    2
Other Side. See spirit world
out-of-body experiences, 121–24
Ovaraith, Rudolph, 114–16

paradise, 40
past lives. See reincarnation
Paul, 164–66
perception, in spirit world, 50, 58,
    110
personality, survival of, 1, 19–21,
    61, 101, 177
pets, 42, 98, 162
plants, 94
pleasure, survival of, 20, 50, 61,
    99–100, 127, 158
Polge, Coral, 18
prayer, power of, 154
Presley, Elvis, 33–35, 188
Price, H. H., 2
progression, 30, 39–41, 105–6,
    179–80
    of animals, 98

of children, 99
and free will, 45, 88
and punishment, 101–2
and reincarnation, 47, 150
psychic phenomena, acceptance
of, 1–2, 4–5
psychics. *See* mediums
Purgatory, 39

reality, of spirit world, 50, 81, 146
and thoughts, 31, 37, 68
Reid, Beryl, 144–47
reincarnation, 47, 86, 157–59,
162–63, 173–74
and angels, 50–51
of families, 111, 149–50
relationships, 30, 67, 141, 204, 210
sexual, 43–44, 60, 77, 126–27, 189
relaxation, 154
religion, 106, 208
and parapsychology, 2
Riscoe, Johnny, 198
Roberts, Dr., 36–41
Roche, Mrs. C. M., 3
Rogers, Rosanna, 7
Rosemary, 90–96

Sam, 109–13
Sarah, 176–80
Schiebele, Werner, 5
schools, 45, 55, 115
senses, survival of, 19–20, 50
See also pleasure, survival of
Seraphim, 118–19
service, 86, 205
"Seventh Heaven," 38
Sinatra, Frank, 91–93, 142–43
sleep, 45–46, 77–78
Smith, George, 63–70
Solomon, Philip, x–xi, 5, 7–11,
13–18
spirit world
awareness of physical, 148–49
dimension of, 36, 58
existence of, 17, 213–14
guidance from, 152–54
levels of, 38–41, 47–48, 85,
97–98, 126–30, 171–72

light in, 177–78
and out-of-body experiences,
121–24
similarity to physical, 51, 53,
146, 190, 201
suffering, purpose of, 29, 106
suicide, 20, 32, 105–6

talents, survival of, 147
teachers, 54–55, 161
telepathy, 30, 66, 189–90
Teresa, Mother, 52, 73, 205
theaters, 91, 145–46
Theo, 121–24
Thomas, Father, 30–32
Thompson, May, 76–81
thoughts, reality of, 31, 37, 68,
103, 213
time, 28, 77–78, 109, 180, 213
transportation, 46, 62, 115, 199
Travers, Lee, 125–30

UFOs, 172
universities, 45, 115

vehicles. *See* transportation
vibration
of physical world, 153
of spirit world, 58, 149
violence
death by, 20, 32
in spirit world, 126–30, 132–38
visualizations, 213

wars, 66–67
West, Mae, 68
Wilde, Oscar, 18
Winters, Bernie, 196–201
work, 30, 44–45, 54–55, 77, 114
and service, 86, 205

ABOUT THE AUTHORS

Philip Solomon was born in 1951 and discovered his unusual psychic gift at an early age. Since 1970, he has been a working medium, psychic and astrologer in his native Midlands, in England. Extensive radio and television work led to a number of successful books, articles, a newspaper column, and work as a trance medium and psychic.

Professor Hans Holzer, Ph.D., parapsychologist residing in New York, is the author of 124 books, many of them dealing with psychic subjects, including *Life Beyond.*

Hampton Roads Publishing Company

. . . for the evolving human spirit

Hampton Roads Publishing Company
publishes books on a variety of subjects including
metaphysics, health, complementary medicine,
visionary fiction, and other related topics.

For a copy of our latest catalog,
call toll-free, 800-766-8009,
or send your name and address to:

Hampton Roads Publishing Company, Inc.
1125 Stoney Ridge Road
Charlottesville, VA 22902
e-mail: hrpc@hrpub.com
www.hrpub.com